Commercial Law

Fifth Edition

GW00580011

Fifth edition published 2006
by Routledge·Cavendish
2 Park Square, Milton Park, Abingdon, Oxon, OX14 4RN

Simultaneously published in the USA and Canada
by Routledge·Cavendish
270 Madison Ave, New York, NY 10016

*Routledge·Cavendish is an imprint of the Taylor & Francis Group,
an informa business*

© 2006 Routledge·Cavendish

First edition published by Cavendish Publishing 1997
Second edition published by Cavendish Publishing 1999
Third edition published by Cavendish Publishing 2002
Fourth edition published by Cavendish Publishing 2004

Typeset in Helvetica by Flcrence Production Ltd, Stoodleigh, Devon
Printed and bound in the UK by Ashford Colour Press, Gosport

British Library Cataloguing in Publication Data
A catalogue record for this book is available from the British Library

Library of Congress Cataloging in Publication Data
A catalog record for this book has been requested

ISBN10: 1-84568-019-7

ISBN13: 978–1–84568–019–0

Contents

1 Definition of contract of sale of goods

Only contracts of sale of goods are governed by the Sale of Goods Act 1979. According to s 2:

> A contract of sale of goods is a contract by which the seller transfers or agrees to transfer the property in goods to the buyer for a money consideration, called the price ...

The basic notion is that a contract of sale of goods is a means of transferring property (meaning ownership) from one person to another. There are other means of doing this. Clearly, making someone a gift or leaving someone a bequest by will are alternatives. There are also other types of contract which may involve transferring ownership and/or possession of goods. The reason that these other types of contract are not contracts of sale of goods is that one or more ingredients of the above definition is missing. These contracts are, therefore, not governed by the Sale of Goods Act 1979.

Contracts which are not governed by the Sale of Goods Act 1979

Type	Why not sale?	Other relevant legislation
Barter or exchange	No money consideration	Sections 2–5 of the Supply of Goods and Services Act 1982
Services	Substance of contract, not the passing of property in goods	Sections 2–5 and 12–16 of the Supply of Goods and Services Act 1982
Hire purchase	No commitment by hirer to accept transfer of property in goods	Sections 8–11A of the Supply of Goods (Implied Terms) Act 1973; Consumer Credit Act 1974

Hire	No provision for transfer of property in goods	Sections 6–11 of the Supply of Goods and Services Act 1982
Sale of land	Land is not within the definition of goods	See *Principles of Land Law*, 4th edn, 2002, by Martin Dixon

Contract of sale of goods

Contracts not governed by the Sale of Goods Act 1979

2 Passing of property and risk

Classification of the contract

Any contract of sale of goods will be one of three types.

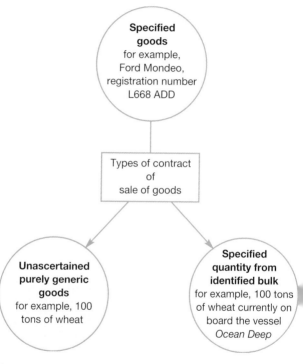

Specific goods

These are goods identified and agreed upon at the time the contract is made (s 61). Thus, the goods are specific goods only if it is possible, at the time the contract is made, to identify the particular goods which are being sold (*Kursell v Timber*

perators (1927)). Property passes when the parties intended it
. Failing a clear indication (either by words or conduct) by the
arties as to when they intend property to pass, the following
les (from s 18) apply.

Section 18, rule number	Applicable circumstances	Time when property passes
1	Unconditional contract for sale of goods in deliverable state	On the making of the contract
2	Seller is bound to do something to the goods to put them into deliverable state	When the thing is done and the buyer has notice that it has been done
3	Sale of goods in a deliverable state and the seller is bound to weigh, measure, test or do something else in order to ascertain the price	When the thing is done and the buyer has notice that it has been done
4	Goods are delivered on approval or sale or return or other similar terms	When buyer signifies approval or acceptance or otherwise adopts the transaction or retains the goods beyond the fixed time for their return or, if there was no fixed time, beyond a reasonable time

Purely generic unascertained goods

These are goods which are not within the definition of specific
goods and which are not sold as an identified quantity out of a
specific bulk. No property can pass in them until they have

become ascertained (s 16). Once the goods have become ascertained, property passes when the parties intend it to pass (s 17). Failing a clear expression by the parties as to when they intend property to pass, the following rules (from s 18) apply. These sections form a hierarchy. Section 16 must be considered first, then s 17, then s 18.

Section 18, rule number	Requirements for property to pass
5(1)	1 Goods of the contract description and in a deliverable state are unconditionally appropriated to the contract by one party; and
	2 the other party assents, expressly or impliedly, to that appropriation either before or after it is made
5(2)	1 In pursuance of the contract, the seller, without reserving the right of disposal, delivers the goods to the buyer or to a carrier for the purpose of transmission to the buyer; and
	2 the buyer assents, expressly or impliedly, to that appropriation either before or after it is made

Unconditional appropriation of the goods is said to occur when one party, usually the seller, does more than merely set aside the goods intended for use to fulfil the contract, but attaches the goods irrevocably to the contract (*Federspiel v Twigg* (1957)). Handing them over (without reserving a right of disposal) to an independent carrier to transport them to the buyer is thus usually a very clear unconditional appropriation (s 18, r 5(2)). It will not be an unconditional appropriation, however, if the goods destined for the buyer remain unascertained, for example, if some of the goods handed over to the carrier are to be delivered to one buyer and some to another, leaving it to the carrier to decide which are to be delivered to which buyer (*Healey v Howlett* (1917)).

Specified quantity out of identified bulk

The buyer cannot become the owner of any particular goods out of the bulk until the particular goods have become ascertained. In this respect, the rules are the same as they are in the case of purely generic, unascertained goods (see above). However, under s 20A it is possible for the buyer to obtain a share in the ownership of the bulk. He or she becomes owner in common of the bulk, that is, property is acquired in the form of an undivided share in the bulk. This occurs only if and when the buyer pays the price, or part of it. The buyer's share is 'such share as the quantity of goods paid for and due to the buyer out of the bulk bears to the quantity of goods in the bulk'.

Of course, if the bulk becomes reduced to (or to less than) the quantity of goods the buyer contracted to buy, then, unless some other buyer also has an interest in the bulk, the whole of the bulk will belong to the buyer. It will be ascertained and appropriated by exhaustion. In that case, the buyer will cease to have merely an undivided share in the bulk but will now be complete owner of the now identified remainder of the bulk (s 18, r 5(3)).

Suppose that buyer A has agreed to buy 600 of the 1,000 widgets stored in a particular warehouse at an agreed price of £2 per widget. The following table of examples indicates the extent of buyer A's proprietary interest in the goods.

Example number	Amount paid by buyer A	Quantity of widgets paid for by buyer A	Quantity of widgets sold by the seller (of the 1,000 bulk) and delivered to other buyers	Extent of buyer A's interest in the bulk
1	£600	300	0	30%
2	£1,200	600	0	60%
3	£1,200	600	200	75%
4	£1,200	600	400	100%
5	£1,200	600	600	100%

Note that, in example 3, the bulk has been reduced by 200 widgets so that buyer A has an interest amounting to 600 out of 800, that is, 75%. Similarly, in example 4, the bulk has been reduced to 600 so that buyer A has an interest amounting to 600 out of 600, that is, 100%. Assuming that there is no other buyer to whom goods are due out of the bulk, then, as soon as the bulk was reduced to 600, buyer A became the outright owner of the whole of the bulk.

Example 5 deals with a situation where, before delivery of any of the goods to buyer A, the seller has sold and delivered 600 widgets (that is, 200 more than there should have been) to another buyer or buyers. This has reduced the bulk to 400 widgets. Clearly, buyer A is now the complete owner of 100% of that reduced bulk. None of the goods which have been sold and delivered to the other buyers can be claimed, since, provided each was *bona fide* and unaware of buyer A's interest in the bulk, they will have obtained good title because buyer A is deemed to consent to a delivery of goods to another co-owner (s 20B). Buyer A does, however, have a claim against the seller for breach of contract, because the seller cannot now comply with the contract by which he undertook to supply buyer A with

0 widgets out of that specified stock. For the buyer's rights hen the wrong quantity is delivered, see p 75, below.

assing of risk

) Where delivery of the goods is delayed through the fault of either party, then any loss of the goods or damage to them, which might not have occurred but for such fault, falls on the party at fault (s 20(2)) (*Demby Hamilton Ltd v Barden* (1949)).

b) Where either of the parties is negligent as a bailee of the goods, then any loss occasioned by that negligence falls upon that party (s 20(3)) (*Wiehe v Dennis Bros* (1913)).

c) The parties may agree upon when the risk passes from seller to buyer (s 20(1)) (*Bovington & Morris v Dale & Cole Ltd* (1902)).

d) Unless otherwise agreed, risk passes to the buyer when property in the goods passes to the buyer (s 20(1)), except that different rules apply in the situation where the buyer has an undivided share in an identified bulk. But where the buyer deals as a consumer, the goods remain at the seller's risk until they are delivered to the consumer.

11

Passing of risk – undivided share of bulk

Unless one of rules (a)–(c) above applies, the position is as follows. First, if the buyer has not paid any of the price, the buyer has no property rights in the bulk and risk remains with the seller. If the buyer has paid some or all of the price, the buyer will have an undivided share in the bulk. In that situation, any accidental loss or damage is regarded as falling first on the share of the bulk which had been retained by the seller (s 20A(3)). Suppose the bulk consists of 1,000 widgets and suppose that the seller has agreed to sell, out of that bulk, 200 to X and 300 to Y. Suppose also that X and Y have each paid the agreed price in full and neither has taken delivery. The following table illustrates the outcome of different scenarios.

Example number	Number of widgets destroyed/ damaged/ lost	Incident	Outcome
1	500	Some of bulk are stolen	Seller bears all the loss
2	600	Some of bulk are stolen	Seller bears loss of 500, X bears loss of 40 and Y bears loss of 60
3	1,000	Accidental fire. No widgets burnt. All equally damaged by smoke	Seller bears half the loss. X bears one-fifth and Y bears three-tenths of the loss

Retention of title clauses

A retention of title clause is used to protect the seller in the situation where the goods have been delivered to the buyer and the buyer becomes insolvent without having paid in full. It is designed to enable the seller to assert a right to the goods in priority to other creditors of the insolvent buyer. At its simplest, it will provide that the property in the goods will not pass to the seller until the seller has paid the price. The risk from the seller's point of view is that the buyer might, before becoming insolvent, have done one of the following:

- paid the seller the price of the goods but not paid the seller other debts owed by the buyer to the seller under other contracts;

- used the goods in a manufacturing process;

- sold the goods.

Thus, the retention of title clause may seek to cover these eventualities.

All liabilities clauses

The first eventuality just mentioned can effectively be covered by an all liabilities retention of title clause, which provides that the property in the goods supplied under the contract will not pass to the buyer until the buyer has paid in full the price payable under this contract and all other debts owing by the buyer to the seller (*Armour v Thyssen* (1990)).

Manufactured goods

Attempts have been made to enable a clause to cover the second eventuality by providing that, when the goods are incorporated via a manufacturing process into another new product, the seller becomes owner of the new product. Such attempts do not work, because the seller is no longer retaining title to the goods sold by the seller but is claiming title over some new goods produced by the buyer. Such a clause creates a charge, in favour of the seller, over the new product which is property of the buyer. That being so, the charge is void unless registered as a charge (s 365 of the Companies Act 1985). Also, the seller usually cannot claim title to the goods originally supplied because they will have lost their identity, as in *Re Peachdart* (1983), where leather had been sold which the buyer had then manufactured into handbags. If, however, the goods originally supplied have not lost their identity, and can be easily detached from other goods, then the seller can claim them under a retention of title clause (*Hendy Lennox v Grahame Puttick* (1984)).

Proceeds of sale

Usually, a retention of title clause will contemplate and authorise the buyer to resell the goods and pass on good title to the new buyer. Thus, the original seller will at that point lose the title to them (s 25). The retention of title clause may provide that, in that case, the original seller will have a proprietary interest in the proceeds of sale received by the buyer. Such a clause has been held to work in only one case: *Aluminium Industrie Vaasen v Romalpa Aluminium Ltd* (1976). However, unless the clause gives the seller complete rights over the proceeds and does not limit them to the amount of the debt owing by the buyer to the seller, it is likely to be regarded as a charge over the buyer's property and will thus be void unless registered (*Pfeiffer GmbH v Arbuthnot Factors* (1988)).

Simple retention of title clause – examples

The following examples illustrate the operation of a valid simple retention of title clause in relation to goods which have been supplied by the seller and not sold or used up by the buyer in a manufacturing process or in any other way. The examples all assume that the clause is not an 'all liabilities' clause and that the buyer has agreed to pay £10,000 for the goods. They assume that, on the buyer's insolvency and liquidation or bankruptcy, the seller is entitled to the goods unless the price has already been paid in full. They are based on the approach set out in *Clough Mill v Martin* (1985).

Example number	Amount of price paid by buyer £	Value of goods as realised on resale by seller £	Amount (if any) of refund due to buyer £	Amount (if any) of price still to be paid by buyer £
1	10,000	0	0	0
2	0	10,000	0	0
3	0	8,000	0	2,000
4	1,000	8,000	0	1,000
5	0	12,000	0	0
6	2,000	12,000	2,000	0
7	1,000	12,000	1,000	0
8	3,000	12,000	3,000	0
9	2,000	9,000	1,000	0

n example 1, the seller would not be entitled to retake the goods, since property will have passed to the buyer on the buyer paying the price in full. The other examples illustrate the following principles:

- Out of the proceeds of resale by the seller, the seller must reimburse the buyer the amount of any part payment already made.

- Before making that reimbursement, the seller is entitled to deduct any loss he has made on the resale.

- Subject to (a) above, the seller is entitled to keep any profit made on the resale, because he resells as owner.

- If any part payment and the proceeds of resale are together less than the original purchase price agreed by the buyer, the buyer is liable to the seller for the shortfall (in example 4, £1,000) – though the seller will be an unsecured creditor as to this shortfall.

3 Void and frustrated sale of goods contracts

The ordinary contract rules relating to mistake and frustration apply to sale of goods contracts. There are, however, specific provisions in ss 6 and 7 of the Sale of Goods Act 1979 about the perishing of specific goods (*Couturier v Hastie* (1856)).

Events before the contract is made

In the case of a contract for the sale of specific goods, if the goods have, unknown to the seller, perished before the contract is made, the contract is void (s 6). This is no more than what the rule would be at common law. Because the contract is concerned with the sale of something which, unknown to the parties, does not exist, it is a contract about nothing.

The rule applies equally (unless the contract is severable) even if only some of the goods have perished – see *Barrow Lane and Ballard v Phillips* (1929) – where some of the goods had apparently already been stolen before the contract was made.

The rule does not apply, however, if the contract was for the sale, not of specific goods (for example, 'the seller's current stock of 100 tons of hazelnuts'), but only of purely generic unascertained goods (for example, '100 tons of hazelnuts'). If the contract was for the sale of unascertained goods out of an identified bulk, then s 6 would not apply, but the contract would nevertheless be void at common law if the identified bulk had, unknown to the seller, ceased to exist at the time the contract was made.

Events after the contract is made

In the case of a contract for the sale of specific goods, where, without the fault of the buyer or the seller, the goods perish after the contract is made and before the risk has passed to the buyer, the contract is avoided (s 7). This mirrors the common law rule that the contract becomes frustrated when, after it is made and through the fault of neither party, it becomes impossible or illegal to perform. Thus, a contract for the sale of unascertained goods from an identified source (for example, '10 tons of wheat to be grown on Blackacre') will be frustrated at common law if, contrary to expectations and through the fault of neither party, Blackacre suffers an unforeseeable blight and produces no crop (*Howell v Coupland* (1876)). If it produces a smaller crop but still enough to enable the seller to supply the contract quantity, the contract will not be frustrated. If it produces a smaller crop so that the seller can supply some but not all of the contract quantity, the seller should offer the buyer the option of either taking the lesser quantity at the contract rate or of not taking any (*Sainsbury v Street* (1972)).

The doctrine of frustration can apply where the contract is for the sale of a specified quantity from an identified bulk, for example, if the identified bulk perishes after the contract is made. If, however, the buyer has paid the price and thus obtained an undivided share in the bulk, then the risk may already have passed to him according to the principles already outlined (see above). In that case, those principles apply and the contract is not frustrated. Even if the buyer has not paid the price, in the case of unascertained goods from an identified bulk, the contract will in any event not be frustrated if the quantity of goods which perish is such that the seller is still able to fulfil the contract from the bulk.

The Law Reform (Frustrated Contracts) Act 1943 applies to contracts frustrated at common law but not to contracts avoided by s 7 of the Sale of Goods Act 1979. In the latter case, the buyer is entitled to recover any of the price already paid, provided that they have suffered a total failure of consideration, but they do not have to make any payment for expenses incurred by the seller in performing the contract. In the former case, the buyer is entitled to his money back, irrespective of whether there has been a total failure of consideration, but may be required to compensate the seller for any use the buyer has had of the goods, or for expenses incurred by the seller in performing the contract.

Effect of goods perishing	Goods perish before contract is made	Goods perish after contract is made
1 Contract for sale of specific goods	Contract may be void by s 6	Contract may be avoided by s 7
2 Contract for sale of unascertained goods from identified source	Contract may be void at common law	Contract may be frustrated at common law
3 Contract for sale of purely generic unascertained goods	Contract is neither void nor frustrated	Contract is neither void nor frustrated

4 Seller is not the owner

General rule

Someone who does not have title to the goods, and is not authorised by the owner to sell them, cannot pass on good title to them. *Nemo dat quod non habet* – no one can give something he has not got.

Exceptions to *nemo dat*

When one of the following exceptions applies, someone without title and without authority to do so can confer good title.

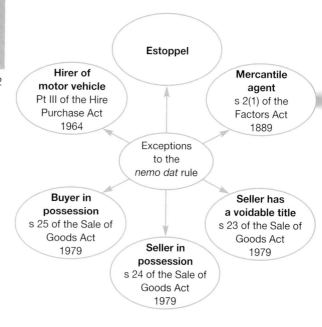

stoppel

The true owner may be estopped (that is, stopped) from asserting that good title has been passed on if the following requirements are all satisfied:

The true owner represented that the seller was the owner or had the owner's authority to sell. (Note that merely letting someone have possession of your goods does not amount to such a representation. That is still the case, even if it is a motor vehicle and you leave him in possession of its registration book as well – *Central Newbury Car Auctions v Unity Finance* (1957).)

The representation was made negligently or intentionally.

The innocent purchaser relied on the representation and bought (not merely agreed to buy) the goods.

Mercantile agent

A mercantile agent is an 'agent having in the customary course of his business as such agent authority either to sell goods or to consign goods for the purpose of sale, or to buy goods, or to raise money on the security of goods' (s 1(1) of the Factors Act 1889; see now s 26 of the Sale of Goods Act 1979).

In addition, in order to be a mercantile agent, the person must be:

independent from the person for whom he or she is agent;

acting as agent by way of business; and

authorised to deal with goods in his or her own name without disclosing the agency.

Before a mercantile agent can pass on good title to someone else's goods (under s 2 of the Factors Act 1889), the following requirements must all be satisfied:

the mercantile agent must be in possession of the goods (or documents of title);

- he must have that possession in his capacity as mercantile agent;

- he must have that possession with the consent of the owner;

- in selling the goods, he must have been acting in the normal course of business of a mercantile agent;

- the purchaser must buy them in good faith, without knowledge of the agent's lack of authority.

A car dealer who has possession of a car for the purpose of repair or servicing would not be in possession in his capacity as mercantile agent. He would be, however, if he had possession for the purpose of seeing what offers he could secure from potential buyers of the car.

Note that, in the case of a motor vehicle, the agent must be in possession not only of the vehicle but also of the registration document; the possession of these items must be with the consent of the owner (*Pearson v Rose and Young* (1950)). Apparently, the same requirement extends also to the possession of the ignition key (*Stadium Finance v Robbins* (1962)). The requirement is that the mercantile agent is in possession 'with the consent of the owner'. This requirement is not satisfied where the mercantile agent obtains possession by means of a trick without the owner's consent. It would, however, be satisfied where the consent of the owner was secured by a deception or fraud.

Seller with voidable title – s 23 of the Sale of Goods Act 1979

A number of cases learnt in the law of contract illustrate situations where a buyer (usually a rogue) has bought goods under a voidable contract, for example, *Phillips v Brooks* (1919) and *Lewis v Averay* (1971). The contract is voidable, usually, because of the fraud of the buyer. The buyer can nevertheless pass on good title provided:

the contract has not been avoided at the time the goods are resold; and

they are sold to someone who takes in good faith and without notice of his defect in title.

This does not apply to the situation where the rogue has acquired the goods under a contract which is void (*Cundy v Lindsay* (1878)).

Even where the contract is voidable, the rule does not apply once the contract has been 'avoided'. It will be avoided once the original seller (that is, the person who sold the goods to the rogue) has shown a definite intention to avoid the contract; he will normally be regarded as doing that when he informs the police (*Car and Universal Finance v Caldwell* (1965)). Where, after the original seller has done that, the rogue subsequently sells the item to an innocent purchaser, the latter will not get good title by virtue of s 23. The innocent purchaser, may however, get a good title under s 25, which deals with the situation where goods are sold by a 'buyer in possession' (see below).

Seller in possession – s 24 of the Sale of Goods Act 1979

A buyer, especially a buyer who has paid for the goods, takes a risk if the goods are left with the seller. The risk is that the seller will sell the goods to another buyer. The first buyer may well find that the title is lost to the second buyer.

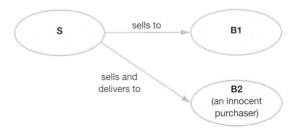

In this example, B1 has bought from S and obtained good title. Nevertheless, S may well have later passed good title to B2, thereby depriving B1 of his title.

A seller will pass on good title under s 24 if the following requirements are satisfied:

- the seller, having sold to the first buyer, continues or is in possession of the goods (or documents of title);
- the seller makes an agreement to sell, pledge or otherwise dispose of the goods or actually sells, etc, the goods;
- the seller delivers the goods under this latter transaction;
- the person taking the goods under this transaction receives the goods in good faith and without notice of the previous sale.

If these requirements are satisfied, the person taking the goods gets a title as good as that of the seller and the original buyer loses the title which had passed to him. The original buyer can sue the seller for breach of contract.

Buyer in possession – s 25 of the Sale of Goods Act 1979

A seller who agrees to sell goods and parts with them to the buyer without first getting paid takes a risk. The risk is that the buyer will dispose of them without having paid the seller. Even if property (that is, title) has not passed from the seller to the buyer, the buyer is able to pass on good title by virtue of s 25 (also s 9 of the Factors Act 1889). The seller will be able to sue the buyer for the price, but will be unable to recover the goods.

In this example, M is a buyer in possession and, if the requirements of the section are met, will pass on good title to N, thereby depriving L of the title.

he buyer will pass on good title provided the following
quirements are satisfied:

the buyer is a 'buyer in possession' of the goods (or
documents of title). A buyer is someone who has bought or
agreed to buy. Someone who has obtained the goods under
a hire purchase agreement is not a 'buyer' (*Helby v Matthews*
(1895)), nor is someone who has obtained the goods under a
conditional sale agreement which is a regulated agreement
within the meaning of the Consumer Credit Act 1974 (s 25(2)
of the Sale of Goods Act 1979);

the buyer obtained possession of the goods (or
documents of title) with the consent of the seller;

the buyer makes a transaction selling, pledging or otherwise
disposing of the goods. In *Re Highway Foods International
Ltd* (1995) it was held that no title will be passed if the buyer
in possession merely *agrees* to sell the goods to the second
buyer.

the buyer delivers the goods (or documents of title) under
that transaction;

the person taking them receives them in good faith without
notice of the rights of the original seller;

(possibly) the buyer in possession, in disposing of the goods,
acted in the way he would have acted if he was a mercantile
agent selling in the ordinary course of business (*Newtons of
Wembley v Williams* (1965)).

The title conferred by this provision is a title only as good as
that of the seller who entrusted possession of the goods to the
'buyer in possession' (*National Mutual General Insurance
Association v Jones* (1968)).

In the example over the page, K steals the item from J and sells
it to L. L agrees to sell it to M subject to a term that property is
not to pass to M until M has paid L the price. Before paying the

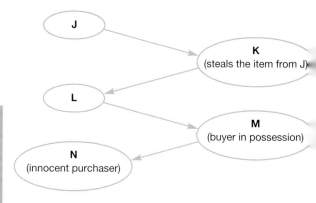

price, M sells and delivers the car to N, an innocent purchaser. By pointing to the fact that he bought from a buyer in possession, N cannot defeat the rights of J.

Motor vehicle sold by hire purchaser

Someone who has goods under a hire purchase agreement or a conditional sale agreement will not normally have good title until his payments have been completed under the agreement. He thus has no title to pass on. However, Pt III of the Hire Purchase Act 1964 has made an exception to *nemo dat*. Thus, in the case of a motor vehicle, the hire purchase (or conditional sale) customer can pass on good title to a private purchaser, even though it is not his to pass on. The following requirements must be satisfied for this to happen:

- the person selling must be someone who has the vehicle under a hire purchase or conditional sale agreement (it makes no difference whether or not the agreement is one which is regulated by the Consumer Credit Act 1974);

- the goods must be a motor vehicle;

- the purchaser must be a 'private' purchaser, not a trader (or finance house) carrying on business in the motor trade;

- the private purchaser must be *bona fide* and unaware of any relevant hire purchase or conditional sale agreement;

- the transaction by which the private purchaser acquires the vehicle must be a contract of sale or of hire purchase.

If the hire purchaser sells the car to a trade (not a private) purchaser, then the first private purchaser thereafter can obtain good title.

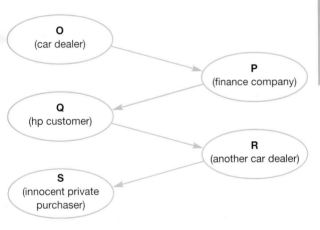

In this example, O has sold the car to P, a finance company which has supplied the car on hire purchase terms to Q. Q, before completing his hire purchase payments, has sold the car to R who has in turn sold it to S. Until R sold the car to S, it belonged to P. However, S gets P's title because S is the first private purchaser and buys in good faith.

The private purchaser will, however, secure only as good a title as that of whoever supplied the vehicle to the hire purchase customer under the hire purchase agreement.

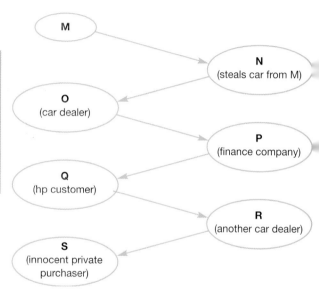

This example is the same as the last except that, before O, we now know that O bought the car from N who had stolen it from M. That being so, O and, therefore, P never had good title to the car. Under the Hire Purchase Act 1964, S can get a title only as good as P's. Thus, M retains the title to the car.

5 Contract terms as to title

Implied condition as to title – s 12 of the Sale of Goods Act 1979

It is an implied condition of a contract of sale of goods that the seller has the right to sell the goods. If he does not, the buyer has the right to reject the goods and recover the purchase price. He is entitled to do this even if he has had possession and enjoyed the use of the goods for some months before discovering that the seller had no title to sell (*Rowland v Divall* (1923)).

Feeding the title

It may happen that the seller does not have title at the time the goods are sold and delivered, but that title is acquired at some later stage.

In the above example, P, who has not completed the hire purchase payments to O, sells the goods to Q who then sells them to R. P is liable to Q for breach of the implied condition as to title. Equally, Q is liable to R for the same reason. If, at some later stage, P completes the hire purchase payments to O, P will acquire good title which will immediately be 'fed' down the line of purchasers to R (*Butterworth v Kingsway Motors* (1957)). Until that happens, R is entitled to reject the goods and reclaim the purchase price from Q. If the goods have not already been rejected, then, after the title has been fed, R loses the right to reject the goods but may claim damages. The damages will be the difference between the value of the goods when he should have got good title (when he bought them) and when he actually got title (when it was fed). Of course, if R rejected the car (before title was fed), then Q could have immediately rejected the car also and reclaimed the purchase price from P.

t may be that the goods were a motor vehicle and that Q
was an innocent private purchaser. In that case, Q will have
obtained good title when the car was purchased from P (that
s, by virtue of Pt III of the Hire Purchase Act 1964). In that
case, Q would not be liable to R for breach of the condition
as to title. Nevertheless, Q would still have a claim against
P for breach of the implied term as to title (*Barber v NWS Bank*
(1996)).

Alternatively, it could happen that Q was a trade purchaser
and that R was an innocent private purchaser. In that case,
R would have obtained good title when the car was bought
(by virtue of the Hire Purchase Act 1964). Again, however,
that would not affect his right to reject the car and recover
the price or to claim damages from Q.

Implied warranties – s 12 of the Sale of Goods Act 1979

There are implied warranties that:

- the goods are free from encumbrances not disclosed
  or known to the buyer before the contract is made;
  and

- the buyer will enjoy quiet possession of the goods,
  apart from disturbance by virtue of any charge or
  encumbrance disclosed or known to the buyer when
  the contract was made.

If one of these terms is broken, the buyer may sue for
damages. They could be broken if, for example, the labelling
of the goods infringed a trade mark (*Niblett v Confectioners'
Materials* (1921)) or if the use of the goods would infringe
someone's patent. This is the case even if the patent was
taken out after the goods were sold (*Microbeads v Vinhurst
Road Markings* (1975)).

Exclusion of terms in s 12 of the Sale of Goods Act 1979

It is, in principle, not possible to exclude the provisions of s 12. Any exclusion is rendered ineffective by the Unfair Contract Terms Act 1977. However, s 12 itself permits a situation where the parties intend that the seller should transfer only such title as he has. This allows a seller, who has reason to doubt whether his title is good, to sell the goods. He will not be in breach of any of the terms of s 12 provided he discloses all charges and encumbrances known to him and, presumably, discloses his reasons for doubting that he has good title. This could arise, for example, if the claim to the goods is only by virtue of having found them.

Other types of contract

The implied terms explained above, in contracts of sale of goods, have their counterparts in other types of contract, such as contracts of hire purchase, barter, hire, etc. For the relevant legislation, see the table on p 2.

6 Misrepresentation

An actionable misrepresentation is an untrue statement of fact made by one party (usually the seller) to the other party (usually the buyer) before the contract is made, which is one of the reasons the other party enters the contract. (It will be assumed in the text from now on that it is the seller who has made the misrepresentation.)

Types of misrepresentation

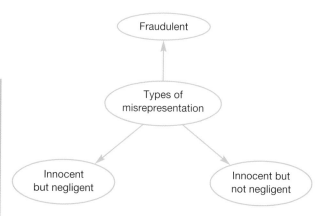

Remedies for misrepresentation

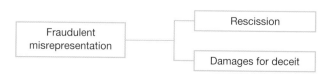

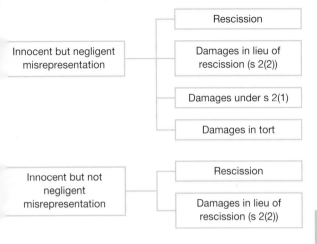

Rescission

The right to rescission of the contract exists independently of any statute. There are bars, any one of which may prevent rescission being available. The three most significant are: (a) where restitution is impossible, for example, where the buyer has consumed the goods; (b) where the buyer has delayed for more than a reasonable length of time before rescinding the contract; and (c) where a third party acting in good faith has already bought the goods (see s 23 of the Sale of Goods Act 1979, on p 24). In the case of a fraudulent representation, the reasonable length of time does not start until the buyer has become aware of the misrepresentation. In the case, however, of innocent misrepresentation (negligent or not), time begins to run when the contract is made (*Leaf v International Galleries* (1950)). By virtue of s 2(2) of the Misrepresentation Act 1967, the court has the discretion to refuse to grant rescission and to award damages instead. Section 2(2) does not apply where the misrepresentation was made fraudulently.

Damages

In the case of a fraudulent misrepresentation, damages are recoverable for all damage directly flowing from the misrepresentation, irrespective of whether the damage was foreseeable (*Smith New Court Securities v Scrimgeour Vickers (Asset Management)* (1996)). In the case of an innocent but negligent misrepresentation, damages under s 2(1) of the Misrepresentation Act 1967 are awarded on the same basis as are damages for a fraudulent misrepresentation (*Royscot Trust v Rogerson* (1991)).

As long as the misrepresentation was not fraudulent, the court has discretion under s 2(2) to award damages instead of rescission. Apart from this possibility, there is no right to damages for a misrepresentation which was not fraudulent or negligent. However, the court can exercise the power to award damages under s 2(1) even if the right to rescission has been lost, for example, by lapse of more than a reasonable length of time (*Thomas Witter Ltd v TBP Industries Ltd* (1996)). In any case, the burden of proving that a misrepresentation was not negligently made falls on the defendant, who must prove 'that he had reasonable grounds to believe and did believe up to the time the contract was made that the facts represented were true' (s 2(1)).

Liability in tort for misrepresentation

Where the buyer has a claim, as set out above, for a contractual misrepresentation, the buyer will have no reason to rely upon a claim in tort unless he wishes to proceed against someone other than the seller. This is because, in a claim for negligent misstatement in tort (under the principle in *Hedley Byrne v*

Heller (1964)), the burden of proving negligence rests upon the claimant.

Exclusion of liability for misrepresentation

Any clause excluding or limiting liability for misrepresentation is of no effect except to the extent it passes the requirement of reasonableness in the Unfair Contract Terms Act 1977 (s 3 of the Misrepresentation Act 1967).

Misrepresentation – rescission and rejection of goods

You are the buyer under a contract of sale of goods and you wish to know if you can rescind the contract and reject the goods because of a misrepresentation. Refer to the diagram on pp 40–41.

Misrepresentation – rescission and rejection of goods

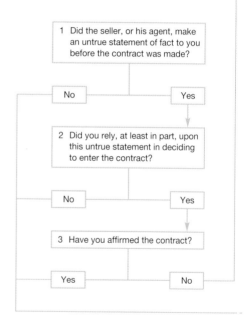

1 Did the seller, or his agent, make an untrue statement of fact to you before the contract was made?

No   Yes

2 Did you rely, at least in part, upon this untrue statement in deciding to enter the contract?

No   Yes

3 Have you affirmed the contract?

Yes   No

4 Is restitution possible (that is, with or without some adjustment to the price)?

No   Yes

5 Was the misrepresentation fraudulent?

Yes   No

6 Has more than a reasonable length of time elapsed since you discovered (or ought to have discovered) that the statement was untrue? Or has a third party acting in good faith already bought the goods?

Yes   No

7 Then you can rescind the contract and reject the goods. (But if the misrepresentation was not fraudulent the court might award s 2(1) damages instead of rescission.) You might also be able to claim damages for misrepresentation, but only if the misrepresentation was either fraudulent or negligent. Alternatively, consider whether you can reject the goods for breach of contract.

8 Has more than a reasonable length of time elapsed since the contract was made? Or has a third party acting in good faith already bought the goods?

No   Yes

9 Then you cannot rescind the contract for misrepresentation, but consider whether you can reject the goods for breach of contract. (You may have a claim for damages for misrepresentation if the answers to the questions in boxes 1 and 2 were both yes, provided that the misrepresentation was not an innocent one made without negligence.)

Rescission and rejection

41

Misrepresentation

7 Express and implied terms

Classification of terms

Each term of a contract must be either:

- an express term of the contract (that is, expressly agreed by the parties); or

- an implied term (one which is implied by law).

Whichever it is, it will be either a *condition* or some other term of the contract. This division is important because the rights of the other party may depend on whether the term is a condition. A term which cannot be classified as a condition or a warranty is 'innominate', but the Sale of Goods Act 1979 implies only conditions or warranties: innominate terms must be express, or implied by some other means.

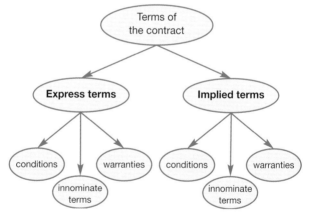

- Whichever type of term is broken, the innocent party is entitled to damages.

- If the term broken is a condition, the innocent party is entitled to regard the contract as repudiated by the guilty party.

- If the term broken is a condition and the innocent party is the buyer, the buyer is entitled to reject the goods and recover any of the price already paid.

- If the term broken is a warranty, the innocent party is not entitled to regard the contract as repudiated and may only claim damages.

- If the term broken is an innominate term, the innocent party is not entitled to regard the contract as repudiated, unless the breach is so serious as to deprive the innocent party of substantially the whole of the benefit of the contract (*Hong Kong Fir Shipping Co v Kawasaki Kisen Kaisha* (1962)).

Implied condition as to description – s 13 of the Sale of Goods Act 1979

Where there is a contract for the sale of goods by description, there is an implied condition that the goods will correspond with the description. See diagram on p 46.

Box 2

The fact that there are words in the contract describing the goods to be supplied does not necessarily mean that those words are part of the description for the purposes of s 13. They will be part of that description if they help to 'identify' the goods (*Ashington Piggeries v Hill* (1971)). However, a term which is not part of the description for the purpose of s 13 is, nevertheless, an express term of the contract and is likely to be regarded as an innominate term. (So the buyer will only be able to treat the contract as repudiated if he has been deprived of substantially the whole benefit of the contract.)

Box 3

If the buyer has placed no reliance upon the seller's description, then that description cannot provide the basis for a claim under s 13 (*Harlingdon Enterprises v Christopher Hull Fine Art* (1991)).

Implied condition as to description

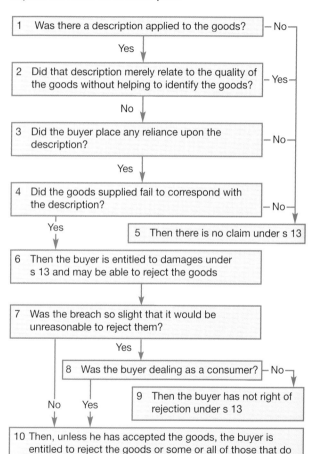

1 Was there a description applied to the goods? — No

Yes

2 Did that description merely relate to the quality of the goods without helping to identify the goods? — Yes

No

3 Did the buyer place any reliance upon the description? — No

Yes

4 Did the goods supplied fail to correspond with the description? — No

Yes

5 Then there is no claim under s 13

6 Then the buyer is entitled to damages under s 13 and may be able to reject the goods

7 Was the breach so slight that it would be unreasonable to reject them?

Yes

8 Was the buyer dealing as a consumer? — No

9 Then the buyer has not right of rejection under s 13

No   Yes

10 Then, unless he has accepted the goods, the buyer is entitled to reject the goods or some or all of those that do not correspond with the description

his is likely to be the case where both parties are aware that the buyer is, and the seller is not, an expert in that description of goods.

Boxes 7–10

For the law on 'slight' breaches of condition and on 'acceptance', see p 58.

Section 14 of the Sale of Goods Act 1979

The implied conditions in s 14, relating to satisfactory quality and fitness for purpose, are implied only if the seller sells 'in the course of a business'. This, however, catches all sales made by businesses, whether or not the sale of such goods is the regular trade of that business (*Stevenson v Rogers* (1999)). (For the facts of this case, see p 70.)

Satisfactory quality – s 14(2) of the Sale of Goods Act 1979

Section 14(2) implies a condition that the goods will be of satisfactory quality when sold by someone selling in the course of a business. See diagram on p 48.

In determining whether the goods are of satisfactory quality, the following (among others) are aspects of the quality of the goods in appropriate cases:

(a) fitness for all the purposes for which goods of the kind in question are commonly supplied;

(b) appearance and finish;

(c) freedom from minor defects;

(d) safety; and

(e) durability.

Satisfactory quality

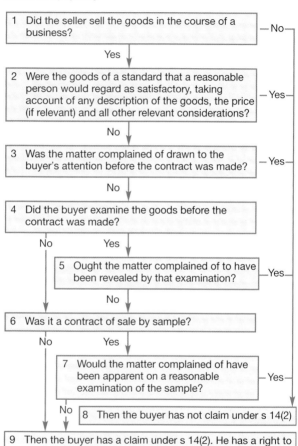

1. Did the seller sell the goods in the course of a business? — No →

   Yes ↓

2. Were the goods of a standard that a reasonable person would regard as satisfactory, taking account of any description of the goods, the price (if relevant) and all other relevant considerations? — Yes →

   No ↓

3. Was the matter complained of drawn to the buyer's attention before the contract was made? — Yes →

   No ↓

4. Did the buyer examine the goods before the contract was made?

   No / Yes

5. Ought the matter complained of to have been revealed by that examination? — Yes →

   No ↓

6. Was it a contract of sale by sample?

   No / Yes

7. Would the matter complained of have been apparent on a reasonable examination of the sample? — Yes →

   No ↓

8. Then the buyer has not claim under s 14(2)

9. Then the buyer has a claim under s 14(2). He has a right to claim damages and may be entitled to reject the goods. For the right of rejection, see p 53

Where the buyer deals as a consumer, the relevant circumstances include any public statements on the specific characteristics of the goods (such as advertising or labelling) made by the seller or the manufacturer (s 14(2D)). This is not the case if the consumer could not have been aware of the statement, or could not have been influenced to buy the goods by the statement, or if the statement was publicly withdrawn or corrected before the consumer bought the goods (s 14(2E)).

- Section 14 was amended by the Sale and Supply of Goods Act 1994. This Act substituted the term 'satisfactory quality' for the previous expression of 'merchantable quality' and it gave the new definition quoted in Box 2 of the flow chart, as well as spelling out the aspects of satisfactory quality just listed.

- In applying the definition to a sale of a motor vehicle, one must recognise that the purposes for which a motor vehicle is commonly bought are not just the purpose of driving it from place to place but of doing so with the appropriate degree of comfort, ease of handling and pride in the vehicle's outward and interior appearance, and a vehicle sold as new should have the performance and finish of an average new vehicle of that model (*Rogers v Parish* (1986)).

- The condition applies equally to goods sold second hand, though in that case minor faults and the normal wear and tear to be expected of goods of the age of those in question will not render the goods of unsatisfactory quality (*Bartlett v Sydney Marcus* (1965)).

- A second hand car which, unknown to the buyer, had been declared an insurance 'write off' might be found for that reason to be of unsatisfactory quality, even if its condition and performance were fine (*Shine v General Guarantee* (1988)).

Satisfactory quality

49

Express and implied terms

Fitness for purpose – s 14(3) of the Sale of Goods Act 1979

Where the seller sells in the course of a business and the buyer makes known to the seller the particular purpose for which the goods are required, there is an implied condition that the goods will be fit for that purpose.

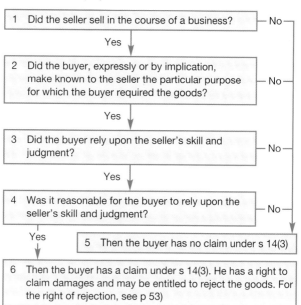

1 Did the seller sell in the course of a business? — No —

Yes ↓

2 Did the buyer, expressly or by implication, make known to the seller the particular purpose for which the buyer required the goods? — No —

Yes ↓

3 Did the buyer rely upon the seller's skill and judgment? — No —

Yes ↓

4 Was it reasonable for the buyer to rely upon the seller's skill and judgment? — No —

Yes ↓

5 Then the buyer has no claim under s 14(3)

6 Then the buyer has a claim under s 14(3). He has a right to claim damages and may be entitled to reject the goods. For the right of rejection, see p 53)

- Where the buyer purchases goods that have only one normal use, for example, a packet of fruit gums, then the mere fact of the purchase makes it known to the seller, by implication, that the buyer requires the goods for that particular purpose (*Priest v Last* (1903)).

- Where the goods are required for some use out of the ordinary, then unless the buyer makes that purpose known, there will be no claim under s 14(3).

- Equally, if the goods are of a type having more than one normal use and they prove not to be fit for one of those uses, the buyer will not be able to rely upon s 14(3), unless it has been made known to the seller that the goods are wanted for the particular use. (It is possible, however, that the buyer would be able, in such a situation, to rely upon s 14(2), where the definition of 'satisfactory quality' refers to one of the aspects of quality being, in appropriate cases, 'fitness for all the purposes for which goods of the kind in question are commonly supplied': see above.)

- The requirement that the goods be reasonably fit for a particular purpose which the buyer has made known to the seller does not require them to be able to cope with some idiosyncrasy of the buyer, or with the circumstances in which the goods are to be used, unless that idiosyncrasy has been made known to the seller (*Slater v Finning* (1996)). Thus, a coat bought by someone for her own use does not have to be suitable for wear by someone with an extra sensitive skin, unless the buyer has intimated that she has extra sensitive skin (*Griffiths v Peter Conway* (1939)). In this matter, it is irrelevant whether she knew that her skin was extra sensitive.

- Liability under s 14(3) – as also under s 14(2) – is strict. It is no defence to the seller that he was not negligent or that he took the utmost care (*Frost v Aylesbury Dairy* (1905)).

- The point (in Boxes 3 and 4 on p 50) about reliance on the seller's skill and judgment is not always straightforward. The buyer may have reasonably relied upon the seller's skill and judgment in one respect but not have done so in another. Thus, a buyer of a tractor for resale in Iran who, to the seller's knowledge, is knowledgeable about what Iranian legal requirements are, is not relying on the skill and judgment of the seller (who is unfamiliar with Iran) to ensure that the

Fitness for purpose

Express and implied terms

tractor fulfils those Iranian legal requirements (*Teheran-Europe v ST Belton* (1968)). He would, however, be relying on the seller's skill and judgment in providing, if that is what the buyer has said is required, a tractor capable of operating in, say, a hard clay terrain. Thus, assuming that the buyer has made known to the seller a particular required purpose, the seller will not be liable if the unsuitability of the goods is outside the sphere of reliance reasonably placed by the buyer on the seller's skill and judgment.

● The requirement that goods reasonably fit the particular indicated purpose is a requirement that they remain reasonably fit for that purpose for a reasonable time after delivery, as long as they remain in the same apparent state and condition as when delivered (*Lambert v Lewis* (1981)).

Sample – s 15 of the Sale of Goods Act 1979

In the case of a contract for sale by sample, there is an implied condition:

● that the bulk will correspond with the sample in quality;

● that the goods will be free from any defect, making their quality unsatisfactory, which would not be apparent on reasonable examination of the sample.

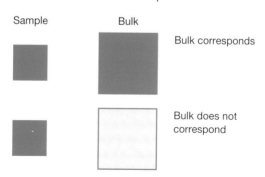

Sample   Bulk

Bulk corresponds

Bulk does not correspond

Where there is a sale by description as well as by sample, the goods must correspond with the description (s 13) as well as with the sample.

Other implied terms

The statutory terms as to title implied by ss 12–15 of the Sale of Goods Act 1979 are the implied terms which it is commonest for a buyer to rely upon. However, it is always open to either party to argue that there was some other term which was implied in the particular contract. This would be done applying the ordinary contract rules for determining whether the term was an implied term of the contract (see *The Moorcock* (1889)):

● Would such a term have been so obvious that the parties felt no need to include it expressly in the contract?

● Was the term necessary to give the transaction such business efficacy as the parties intended?

It is now established that where, as part of the contract, the seller undertakes to despatch the goods to the buyer, there will normally be an implied term that the goods will be in such a state at the time of despatch that they are fit to withstand the rigours of an ordinary journey (*Mash and Murrell v Joseph Emmanual* (1961)).

Rejection of the goods for breach of condition

In principle, the buyer has the right to reject the goods and to reclaim any of the price paid if there is a breach of condition by the seller. Before 1995, there was a general rule, however, that required the buyer to reject all or none of the goods; if the buyer accepted any of the goods, the right of rejection was lost. Apart from that, any breach of condition, however trivial the breach might be, gave the buyer the right of rejection. In these two respects, and also in one or two other respects, the law was changed by amendments to the Sale of Goods Act 1979 by the Sale and Supply of Goods Act 1994.

Rejection of goods – a flow chart

You are the buyer under a contract of sale of goods. The seller is in breach of condition and you wish to know if you can reject the goods.

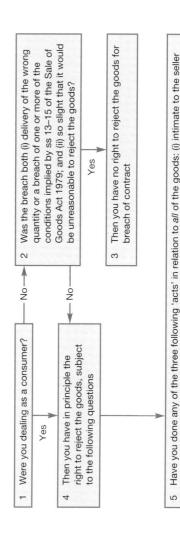

1 Were you dealing as a consumer?

— No →

2 Was the breach both (i) delivery of the wrong quantity or a breach of one or more of the conditions implied by ss 13–15 of the Sale of Goods Act 1979; and (ii) so slight that it would be unreasonable to reject the goods?

Yes ↓

— No →

3 Then you have no right to reject the goods for breach of contract

Yes ↓

4 Then you have in principle the right to reject the goods, subject to the following questions

5 Have you done any of the three following 'acts' in relation to all of the goods: (i) intimate to the seller that you accepted them; (ii) after delivery do any act in relation to them inconsistent with the ownership of the seller; (iii) retain them for more than a reasonable length of time without intimating to the seller that you rejected them?

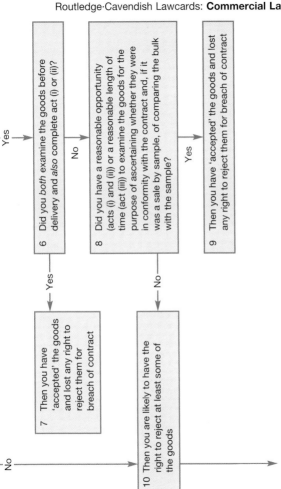

6 Did you *both* examine the goods before delivery and *also* complete act (i) or (ii)?

— Yes →

7 Then you have 'accepted' the goods and lost any right to reject them for breach of contract

↓ Yes

8 Did you have a reasonable opportunity (acts (i) and (ii)) or a reasonable length of time (act (iii)) to examine the goods for the purpose of ascertaining whether they were in conformity with the contract and, if it was a sale by sample, of comparing the bulk with the sample?

→ Yes →

9 Then you have 'accepted' the goods and lost any right to reject them for breach of contract

↓ No

10 Then you are likely to have the right to reject at least some of the goods

— No →

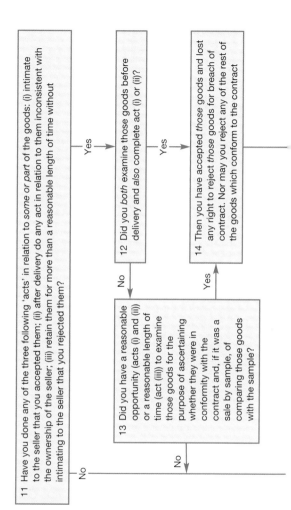

11 Have you done any of the three following 'acts' in relation to *some or part* of the goods: (i) intimate to the seller that you accepted them; (ii) after delivery do any act in relation to them inconsistent with the ownership of the seller; (iii) retain them for more than a reasonable length of time without intimating to the seller that you rejected them?

→ Yes →

12 Did you *both* examine those goods before delivery and *also* complete act (i) or (ii)?

→ Yes →

14 Then you have accepted *those* goods and lost any right to reject *those* goods for breach of contract. Nor may you reject any of the rest of the goods which conform to the contract

No ↓

13 Did you have a reasonable opportunity (acts (i) and (ii)) or a reasonable length of time (act (iii)) to examine those goods for the purpose of ascertaining whether they were in conformity with the contract and, if it was a sale by sample, of comparing those goods with the sample?

Yes ↑ (to box 14)

No ↓

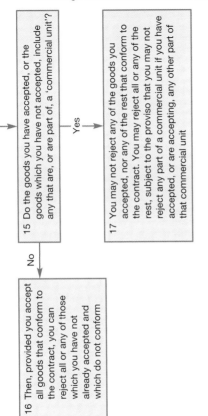

15 Do the goods you have accepted, or the goods which you have not accepted, include any that are, or are part of, a 'commercial unit'?

No → 16 Then, provided you accept all goods that conform to the contract, you can reject all or any of those which you have not already accepted and which do not conform

Yes → 17 You may not reject any of the goods you accepted, nor any of the rest that conform to the contract. You may reject all or any of the rest, subject to the proviso that you may not reject any part of a commercial unit if you have accepted, or are accepting, any other part of that commercial unit

18 Then you may reject all of the goods. Alternatively, you may reject part of the goods provided: (i) that you accept all those that conform to the contract; and (ii) you do not reject any which together with some goods that you are accepting form a 'commercial unit'

Express and implied terms Rejection of the goods

58

Note

In the flow chart, goods are described as conforming to the contract when they are not affected by the breach which gives rise to a right of rejection – and vice versa. The chart assumes that the contract in question was not a severable one and that the breach of condition was not an anticipatory breach.

Trivial breach of condition

The amendments to the Sale of Goods Act 1979, effected by the Sale and Supply of Goods Act 1994, included the insertion of s 15A. Section 15A removes the right to reject goods for breach of condition if the breach is so slight that rejection of the goods would be unreasonable. This restriction on the right to reject applies, however, only to breaches of the conditions implied by ss 13–15 of the Sale of Goods Act 1979 and to breach of the obligation to deliver the correct contract quantity. Even in relation to those implied conditions, it does not apply where the buyer is 'dealing as a consumer' (that is, within the meaning of the Unfair Contract Terms Act 1977). See Boxes 1–3 in the flow chart on pp 54–57.

Rejection of part of the goods

The Sale and Supply of Goods Act 1994 amended s 35 of the Sale of Goods Act 1979 so as to alter the previous rule that, if the buyer accepted any of the contract goods, the buyer thereby lost the right to reject any. Section 35 now allows the buyer to accept part of the goods and remain entitled to reject goods the buyer has not accepted. Thus, the flow chart deals in Boxes 5–9 with the situation where the buyer accepts all the goods and in Boxes 11–17 with the situation where the buyer accepts some of the goods.

There are two qualifications to the buyer's freedom to accept part and reject part of the goods. First, if any goods are accepted, the buyer is not allowed to reject any other of the goods that conform to the contract. Secondly, if any of the oods are a 'commercial unit', acceptance of any part of the goods within that commercial unit is automatically deemed to be an acceptance of all the goods within that commercial unit. A commercial unit means a 'unit division of which would materially impair the value of the goods or the character of the unit' (s 35(7)).

Acceptance – s 35 of the Sale of Goods Act 1979

Acceptance occurs when any one of the three following things occurs:

- the buyer intimates to the seller that the buyer has accepted them;

- the buyer, after delivery of the goods, does any act in relation to the goods which is inconsistent with the ownership of the seller;

- the buyer retains the goods for more than a reasonable length of time without intimating to the seller that the buyer has rejected the goods.

One of the amendments brought about by the Sale and Supply of Goods Act 1994 was that in the first two of the three types of 'acceptance', the buyer will not be deemed to have accepted the goods until the buyer has had a reasonable opportunity of examining them 'for the purpose of ascertaining whether they are in conformity with the contract' (and, if there was a sample, of comparing the bulk with the sample). Similarly, in the case of the third type of acceptance, whether the buyer has had an opportunity of ascertaining if the goods conform to the contract is a factor in determining whether a reasonable length of time has elapsed. While the buyer is waiting for the seller to provide information as to how complex goods might be repaired, the buyer will not lose the right to reject merely by retaining the goods until the information is communicated. (*Clegg v Olle Andersson* (2003).) But if the way in which the goods could be repaired was obvious, a buyer who delays in rejecting could lose the right to reject by keeping the goods for longer than a reasonable time. (*Jones v Callagher* (2004).)

Also, a buyer will not be deemed to have accepted goods merely because:

- the buyer asks for, or agrees to, their repair;

- the goods are delivered to another under a sub-sale or other disposition.

Product liability – a claim in tort?

Where the buyer has a defective product, the lawyer may well think beyond claims being made for misrepresentation or breach of contract. There are three types of claim in tort that might be considered:

- a claim in negligence under the principle in *Donoghue v Stephenson* (1932);

- a claim for breach of safety regulations, if the product in question was subject to any safety regulations;

- a claim for product liability under Pt I of the Consumer Protection Act 1987.

Each of these claims suffers from the same drawback, which is that these causes of action are available only when the claimant is claiming for loss or damage caused by the defective product. This may well be very valuable when a product has, perhaps, injured the claimant or burnt down his house. These claims in tort are, however, of no use when all that the buyer has to complain about is that the product wears out, does not work properly, is of poor quality, etc. In these cases, the buyer only has his claims for misrepresentation or breach of contract upon which to rely.

Where the product has caused damage to persons or other property, then one of the tort claims mentioned above may well be very useful for the following reasons:

the claim can usually be made against the manufacturer or producer (who may well have more resources than the retailer);

the claim can be made by the party who has suffered the loss (who may not be the buyer);

the claim, unless it is in negligence, is one based on strict liability.

The third of these advantages applies equally, of course, when the buyer is suing the seller relying on one of the conditions implied by s 14 as to satisfactory quality and fitness for purpose.

Implied terms in contracts other than sale of goods

The terms in ss 12–15 of the Sale of Goods Act 1979 are implied only in contracts of sale of goods. However, in analogous contracts, virtually identical terms are implied by other statutory provisions. Thus, for example, there are identical terms implied in hire purchase contracts by the Supply of Goods (Implied Terms) Act 1973. See the table on pp 2–3 for the legislation relevant to other types of contract, such as contracts for services, for barter or exchange and for the hire of goods.

8 Exemption and limitation clauses

To be effective, an exemption clause must clear certain hurdles:

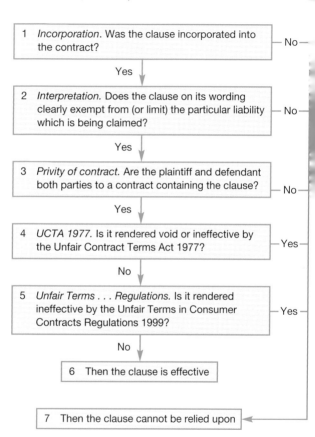

1 *Incorporation.* Was the clause incorporated into the contract? — No —

↓ Yes

2 *Interpretation.* Does the clause on its wording clearly exempt from (or limit) the particular liability which is being claimed? — No —

↓ Yes

3 *Privity of contract.* Are the plaintiff and defendant both parties to a contract containing the clause? — No —

↓ Yes

4 *UCTA 1977.* Is it rendered void or ineffective by the Unfair Contract Terms Act 1977? — Yes —

↓ No

5 *Unfair Terms . . . Regulations.* Is it rendered ineffective by the Unfair Terms in Consumer Contracts Regulations 1999? — Yes —

↓ No

6 Then the clause is effective

7 Then the clause cannot be relied upon ←

Incorporation

In a written contract, any exclusion clause will normally be found within the written words of the contract.

Where the contract is not in writing, the clause may be incorporated by:

- express oral agreement;
- a notice;
- a previous course of dealings between the parties.

For a clause to be incorporated, sufficient reasonable steps must be taken to draw it to the attention of the party whose claims the clause seeks to limit (*Thornton v Shoe Lane Parking* (1971)). The more draconian the clause, the greater the efforts that must be made to bring it to that party's attention. These steps must be taken before the contract is made; a clause cannot be incorporated after the contract has been made (*Olley v Marlborough Court* (1949)).

Interpretation

At one time, there was a rule (asserted in various decisions of the Court of Appeal) that an exclusion clause could not, however it was worded, exclude liability for a 'fundamental' breach of contract. That rule was itself abolished by the decision of the House of Lords in *Photo Production v Securicor Transport* (1980). The approach of the courts in interpreting exclusion clauses now is as follows:

- The clause will not be given a strained meaning in order to limit its effect.
- The clause will be given its ordinary meaning and taken to exclude those liabilities which that meaning suggests.
- Where the clause is genuinely ambiguous, it will be given the meaning which excludes less rather than more liability, that

is, it is construed in the way which least favours the party relying upon it. This is called construing the clause *contra proferentem*.

- The *contra proferentem* approach may not be applied so rigorously where the clause merely purports to limit, rather than exclude, a given liability.

- A clause will not normally be construed as excluding liability for negligence where it does not expressly say so, unless of course exclusion of that liability was clearly intended – as might well be the case where negligence is the only likely head of liability.

The above approach, which is based on the courts giving to a clause the meaning which its wording suggests, does not mean that widely worded clauses will necessarily be effective, because any exclusion clause may be rendered ineffective by the Unfair Contract Terms Act (UCTA) 1977 or by the Unfair Terms in Consumer Contracts Regulations 1999.

Third party rights

Only a party to a contract can be bound by the exclusion terms of that contract, although if a third party wishes to rely on a contract term which he is permitted to enforce under the contract or which is for his benefit, then he is also subject to any exclusion clause which applies to that term (Contracts (Rights of Third Parties) Act 1999). An exclusion clause which purports to confer immunity on a third party can be relied on by him in the event that he is sued by a party bound by the contract (1999 Act). In every case, a third party can derive benefits from a contract term only if he is identified by name, class or description.

Unfair Contract Terms Act 1977

A seller who has sold goods in the course of business wants to know the effect of the UCTA 1977 on an exemption clause.

See table on pp 68–69.

- The effect of the UCTA 1977 depends upon the particular basis of the buyer's claim against the seller.

- Generally, however, the UCTA 1977 has no effect at all where the seller is not someone selling in the course of a business, that is, where the liability is not 'business liability'. Even to this rule, however, there are two exceptions. These are that, even where the seller is not selling in the course of a business:
  - liability under s 12 of the Sale of Goods Act 1979 cannot be excluded; and
  - any clause excluding liability for misrepresentation or for breach of the terms implied by ss 13–15 of the Sale of Goods Act 1979 will have no effect unless it satisfies the Act's requirement of reasonableness.

- The rules of the UCTA 1977 apply to both exemption clauses and clauses which merely seek to limit liability (for example, to a maximum figure).

- In the following treatment of the different bases of liability, it will be assumed: (a) that the liability referred to is 'business liability'; and (b) that by 'exemption clause' is meant 'exemption or limitation of liability clause' and 'exclude' means 'exclude or limit'.

Liability for negligence

- Liability for death or personal injury caused by negligence cannot be excluded.

- Liability for other loss or damage caused by negligence can be excluded but only to the extent that the clause satisfies the requirement of reasonableness.

Liability for misrepresentation

This liability can be excluded but only to the extent that the clause satisfies the requirement of reasonableness.

The effect of UCTA 1977 on an exemption clause

No	What is basis of buyer's claim?	Was seller selling in course of a business?	Was buyer dealing as a consumer?	Clause part of seller's written standard terms of business?	The effect of the UCTA 1977	UCTA 1977 section no.
1	Breach of implied term as to title in s 12	N/A	N/A	N/A	Liability under s 12 cannot be excluded	6
2	Breach of implied terms in ss 13–15	Yes	Yes	N/A	Liability cannot be excluded	6
3	Breach of implied terms in ss 13–15	N/A	No	N/A	Clause is subject to reasonableness requirement	6
4	Breach of a contract term, other than ss 12–15	No	N/A	N/A	UCTA 1977 of no effect	
5	Breach of a contract term, other than ss 12–15	Yes	Yes	N/A	Clause is subject to reasonableness requirement	3

6	Breach of contract term other than ss 12–15	Yes	N/A	Yes	Clause is subject to reasonableness requirement	3
7	Claim in negligence for death or personal injury	Yes	N/A	N/A	Clause cannot exclude this liability	2(1)
8	Claim in negligence for other loss or damage	Yes	N/A	N/A	Clause is subject to reasonableness requirement	2(2)
9	Claim in negligence for death or personal injury or any other loss	No	N/A	N/A	UCTA 1977 of no effect, unless claim falls under one of the heads above	
10	Misrepresentation	N/A	N/A	N/A	Clause is subject to reasonableness requirement	8 (Misrepresentation Act 1967, s 3)

Exemption and limitation

Unfair Contract Terms Act 1977

Liability for breach of terms as to title in s 12

- Liability under s 12 of the Sale of Goods Act 1979 cannot be excluded.

- Note, however, that s 12 itself allows for a lesser liability where the seller is contracting only to pass on such title as the seller actually has (see p 36).

Liability for breach of terms implied by ss 13–15

- Where the buyer is dealing as a consumer, this liability cannot be excluded.

- Where the buyer is not dealing as a consumer, this liability can be excluded but only to the extent that the clause satisfies the requirement of reasonableness.

Was the buyer dealing as a consumer?

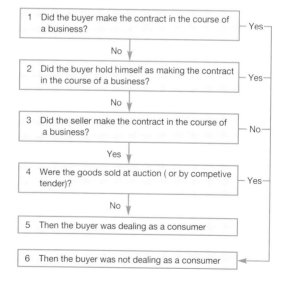

1 Did the buyer make the contract in the course of a business? — Yes

No ↓

2 Did the buyer hold himself as making the contract in the course of a business? — Yes

No ↓

3 Did the seller make the contract in the course of a business? — No

Yes ↓

4 Were the goods sold at auction (or by competive tender)? — Yes

No ↓

5 Then the buyer was dealing as a consumer

6 Then the buyer was not dealing as a consumer

Boxes 2 and 3

There are conflicting Court of Appeal authorities on 'in the course of a business'. In *R and B Customs Brokers v United Dominions Trust* (1988), a shipping brokerage company, which bought a car for its executives to drive round in, was held not to have bought the car in the course of its business (and therefore to have been 'dealing as a consumer') because this was not a type of transaction made *regularly* by the company. In *Stevenson v Rogers* (1999), a fisherman sold his fishing boat five years after he had bought it. He was to buy another to replace it. It was held that 'in the course of a business' was intended to have a wide meaning and to include all sales of goods made by businesses, whether or not the sale of such goods was the regular trade of that business. The fisherman's sale of the boat therefore *was* in the course of his business as a fisherman and thus there was in the contract of sale an implied term that the boat must be of merchantable quality (*now* satisfactory quality). So 'in the course of a business' means one thing when considering s 14 of the Sale of Goods Act 1979 and a different thing when considering whether a person was dealing as a consumer for the purposes of s 12 UCTA 1977. For some time it was doubted whether the phrase could have the two different meanings. However, in *Feldaroll Foundry plc v Hermes Leasing Ltd* (2004) the Court of Appeal confirmed that both *R & B Customs Brokers* and *Stevenson v Rogers* were correctly decided.

Liability for breaches of contract other than ss 12–15 of the Sale of Goods Act 1979

● If the exemption clause was part of the written standard terms of the seller, then liability can be excluded but only to the extent that the clause satisfies the requirement of reasonableness.

● If the buyer was dealing as a consumer, then, irrespective of whether the clause was part of the seller's standard terms,

Unfair Contract Terms Act 1977

Exemption and limitation

71

the liability can be excluded, but only to the extent that the clause satisfies the requirement of reasonableness.

The requirement of reasonableness

The requirement is (s 11 of the UCTA 1977) that the clause 'shall have been a fair and reasonable one to be included, having regard to the circumstances that were, or ought reasonably to have been, known to or in the contemplation of the parties when the contract was made'. A clause will be held to be unreasonable unless the seller shows that it satisfies this test.

Matters to be taken into account include (Sched 2 to the UCTA 1977):

- the relative strength of the bargaining position of the parties;
- alternative ways of meeting the buyer's requirements;
- whether the buyer had an inducement to agree to the clause;
- whether the buyer had an opportunity to enter a similar contract without the clause in question;
- whether the buyer knew, or ought reasonably to have known, of the term;
- whether any condition imposed for the buyer to avoid the effect of the clause was unreasonable;
- whether the goods were processed or manufactured to the special order of the customer.

The judge at first instance will have to balance the various relevant factors to come to a decision as to whether the clause satisfies the requirement of reasonableness. The Court of Appeal or House of Lords will overturn the judge's decision on that matter only if the judge is shown to have proceeded on some wrong principle or to have been plainly and palpably wrong (*George Mitchell v Finney Lock Seeds* (1983)). A very ignificant factor, not perhaps spelt out above, is the 'insurance' factor, whereby the court considers which party it is reasonable to expect to carry the insurance against the risk that has materialised. Thus, when the seller supplied the wrong cabbage seeds which resulted in the crop of the buyer (a farmer) being a total write-off, it was held that it was reasonable to expect the sellers to insure against their liability for that loss. That, coupled with the fact that the sellers had control over which seeds were supplied and the buyer had no way of knowing whether the correct seeds had been supplied, meant that the limitation of liability clause in the seller's contract failed to satisfy the requirement of reasonableness and could not be relied upon by the seller. A clause which requires the buyer to notify the seller within an unreasonable period of time (for example, three days in the case of potato seeds) or else be bound by the seller's limitation of liability is likely to fail the reasonableness requirement.

UCTA 1977 and contracts other than sale of goods

The provisions of the UCTA 1977 apply to other contracts, such as contracts of hire purchase and for services, in the same way as they apply to sale of goods contracts. Thus, the exclusion of liability for terms as to title, description, quality and sample (which are implied by different statutes into the different types of contract just listed) is dealt with in broadly the same way by the UCTA 1977.

The Unfair Terms in Consumer Contracts Regulations 1999

Scope of regulations

The regulations replaced earlier regulations made in 1994. They implement European Directive 93/13. They apply only to consumer contracts, that is, contracts where, in making the contract:

- the seller/supplier of goods or services makes the contract for the purposes of the business; and

- the buyer/customer is an individual who makes the contract for purposes other than business purposes.

'Business' includes trade or profession.

Effect of the regulations

- They require all written terms to be in plain intelligible language. Where there is doubt as to the meaning, the interpretation most favourable to the consumer is to prevail.

- Apart from the latter requirement, the regulations do not apply to the 'core' terms of the contract, that is, terms which:

  - define the main subject matter of the contract; or

  - concern the adequacy of the price or remuneration for the goods or services being supplied.

- Any term which is unfair is of no effect. The rest of the contract, however, is not affected, provided it is capable of subsisting without the term in question.

What is an unfair term?

An unfair term is any term which contrary to the requirement of good faith causes a significant imbalance in the parties' rights under the contract to the detriment of the consumer.

'Good faith' is not defined and, unlike the earlier (1994) regulations, the 1999 regulations do not spell out any relevant factors. In *Director General of Fair Trading v First National Bank plc* (2002) the House of Lords said that good faith here required fair and open dealing. Terms should be clear and legible with no concealed pitfalls or traps.

The regulations contain a long indicative list of clauses likely to be unfair. These include not only exemption clauses, but also clauses which give the seller/supplier rights without compensating rights for the consumer, for example:

- enabling the seller/supplier to raise the price, without giving the buyer a chance to back out if the price rise is too high;

- enabling the seller/supplier to cancel the agreement without penalty without also allowing the customer a similar right;

- automatically extending the duration of the contract, unless the customer indicates otherwise within an unreasonably brief period of time.

Enforcement

The Office of Fair Trading has a duty to consider any complaint made to it that any contract term drawn up for general use is unfair. It is empowered to bring proceedings for an injunction against any business using an unfair term. For the first time, a similar power to apply for such an injunction is given to certain other 'qualifying bodies', including the Data Protection Registrar, the regulators of the privatised public utilities and the Consumers' Association. The Office of Fair Trading often will not need to seek an injunction but will, instead, accept an appropriate assurance from the business in question.

9 Delivery and payment in sale of goods

What is delivery?

Delivery normally means the physical handing over of the goods (or documents of title), though it may be effected by handing over the means of their control, as when the goods are in the hands of a third party who 'attorns', that is, acknowledges that he now holds them for the buyer.

Time of delivery

In a commercial contract, a stipulated time for delivery will normally be 'of the essence', that is, a condition of the contract. If the goods are late being delivered, the buyer will therefore have the right to reject the goods.

Waiver

The buyer may, however, waive his right to reject the goods by, for example, indicating that they will be acceptable if delivered before some new later deadline stipulated. If this is done and the goods are not delivered by the new deadline, the buyer's right to reject the goods will revive (*Rickards v Oppenheim* (1950)). Waiver by the buyer of the right to reject will not deprive the buyer of the right to claim damages for late delivery, normally assessed as the drop (if any) in the market value of the goods between the time when they should have been delivered and their value when in fact they were delivered.

Where no time for delivery is agreed by the parties, the rule in s 28 of the Sale of Goods Act 1979 applies. This is that, unless otherwise agreed, delivery of the goods and payment of the price are concurrent conditions. In that case, the seller must expect to be ready to hand over the goods upon demand and against payment any time after the contract is made.

Place of delivery

Unless otherwise agreed, the place for delivery is 'the seller's place of business, if he has one and, if not, his residence' (s 29 of the Sale of Goods Act 1979).

Delivery of wrong quantity – s 30 of the Sale of Goods Act 1979

Seller tenders the wrong quantity. Can the buyer reject the goods? Unless otherwise agreed, delivery of the wrong quantity is normally a breach of condition entitling the buyer to reject all the goods. However, he does not have to do so.

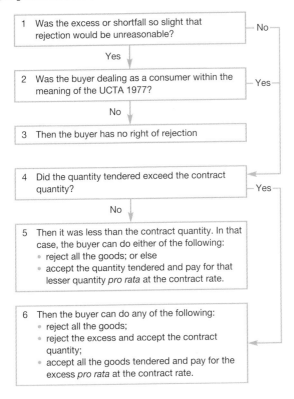

1 Was the excess or shortfall so slight that rejection would be unreasonable? — No

Yes ↓

2 Was the buyer dealing as a consumer within the meaning of the UCTA 1977? — Yes

No ↓

3 Then the buyer has no right of rejection

4 Did the quantity tendered exceed the contract quantity? — Yes

No ↓

5 Then it was less than the contract quantity. In that case, the buyer can do either of the following:
- reject all the goods; or else
- accept the quantity tendered and pay for that lesser quantity *pro rata* at the contract rate.

6 Then the buyer can do any of the following:
- reject all the goods;
- reject the excess and accept the contract quantity;
- accept all the goods tendered and pay for the excess *pro rata* at the contract rate.

Delivery of wrong quantity

79

Delivery and payment

In the case of a severable contract, the above rules are applied separately to each instalment. The usual signs that a contract is severable are that the goods are to be delivered in instalments and each instalment is to be paid for separately.

Payment

- The amount of the price may be fixed by the contract, or may be left to be fixed in a manner agreed by the contract, or may be determined by the course of dealing between the parties. Where the payment is not determined by one of these methods, the buyer must pay a reasonable price (s 8 of the Sale of Goods Act 1979).

- Normally, however, the price is such a fundamental part of the contract that if it is not agreed and not to be determined by one of the listed methods, the contract will be void (*May and Butcher v R* (1934)).

- Unless otherwise stipulated, a contract stipulation as to the date or time of payment will not be a condition of the contract. Thus, lateness in paying does not entitle the seller to regard the contract as repudiated.

- The parties may, however, state that prompt payment is 'of the essence' of the contract, in which case, lateness in payment may be treated by the seller as a repudiation (*Lombard North Central v Butterworth* (1987)).

- Unless otherwise agreed, payment and delivery are concurrent requirements of the contract. This means that:
  - the buyer is not entitled to credit unless it has been agreed; and
  - the buyer is not entitled to demand delivery of the goods unless the buyer is willing to pay at that time.

10 Seller's remedies

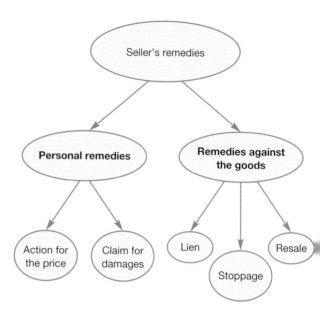

An unpaid seller

- The seller is 'unpaid' unless the whole of the price has been paid or tendered.

- Payment by a cheque or other negotiable instrument is normally a conditional payment only. Thus, if the cheque is dishonoured, the seller is 'unpaid' (s 38 of the Sale of Goods Act 1979).

- Payment by credit or charge card, however, is an absolute and not a conditional payment. So, if the card issuing bank fails to pay the seller, the seller will have no claim against the buyer who paid by the card (*Re Charge Card Services Ltd* (1988)).

Action for the price – s 49 of the Sale of Goods Act 1979

So you wish to know if the seller is entitled to sue for the price:

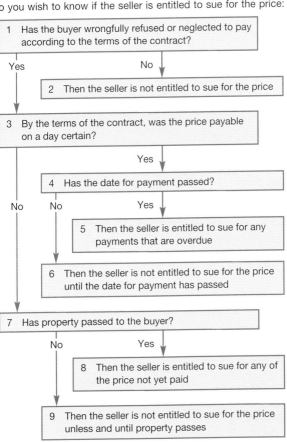

1 Has the buyer wrongfully refused or neglected to pay according to the terms of the contract?

Yes → No →

2 Then the seller is not entitled to sue for the price

3 By the terms of the contract, was the price payable on a day certain?

Yes ↓

4 Has the date for payment passed?

No | No | Yes

5 Then the seller is entitled to sue for any payments that are overdue

6 Then the seller is not entitled to sue for the price until the date for payment has passed

7 Has property passed to the buyer?

No | Yes

8 Then the seller is entitled to sue for any of the price not yet paid

9 Then the seller is not entitled to sue for the price unless and until property passes

- It may be that the parties have agreed that the payment will be paid not on a particular date, but upon the occurrence of some event (for example, the seller completes, or reaches a certain stage in, making the goods). If so, that event will be treated as a 'day certain' (*Workman Clerk v Lloyd Brazileno* (1908)).

- It may be that the parties have agreed that payment will be made in instalments on particular dates (or upon particular events occurring). If so, when the date is reached (or the event occurs) for any one instalment, the seller is entitled to that instalment of the price. The instalment is to be paid on a 'day certain'.

- A seller who sues for the price is suing in debt. The Late Payment of Commercial Debts (Interest) Act 1998 now allows any business to claim interest, calculated at a statutory rate, if a debt is not paid within 30 days of its becoming due.

- Unless otherwise agreed, payment and delivery are concurrent conditions. Therefore, in the absence of contrary agreement, the seller is not entitled to maintain an action for the price unless the seller is ready and willing to deliver.

- If the payment was not due to be made on a 'day certain' and property has not passed, the unpaid seller will not be able to maintain an action for the price.

Damages for non-acceptance – s 50 of the Sale of Goods Act 1979

The seller, even if unable to maintain an action for the price, may be able to maintain an action for damages if the buyer wrongfully refuses to accept and pay for the goods. In this situation, the seller is left with the goods to dispose of.

- In assessing damages, the law assumes that the seller will dispose of the goods on the date of the buyer's wrongful refusal to take delivery.

Thus, the *prima facie* measure of damages is X–Y where:

X = the contract price; and

Y = the market price on the date when the buyer should have taken delivery.

- Thus, if the market price on that date exceeds the contract price, the *prima facie* measure of damages is zero and the seller is entitled only to nominal damages.

- If the seller chooses not to sell the goods in the market immediately, then that is normally irrelevant and the seller takes the risk of the price subsequently falling and takes the benefit if the price subsequently rises.

- The *prima facie* measure of damages does not apply where there is no available market (*Thompson v Robinson* (1955)). In this case, the retail price of a new car was fixed and when the buyer backed out and refused to take delivery, the seller sold the car to another buyer for exactly the same price. However, the result of the buyer backing out was that the seller sold one fewer car than he would have done. Thus, the damages awarded were not the *prima facie* measure (which would have been zero) but the seller's loss of profit (mark up) on one sale. The same reasoning does not apply to the sale of second hand cars; in that case, the *prima facie* measure applies (*Lazenby Garages v Wright* (1976)).

Lien – ss 39–43 of the Sale of Goods Act 1979

The unpaid seller, if still in possession of the goods, is entitled to retain that possession until paid. In the situation where property has already passed to the buyer, this right is termed a lien. Otherwise, it is simply termed a right of retention.

The right exists in each of the following situations:

- where there has been no agreement to allow the buyer credit;

- where the goods were sold on credit but the term of credit has expired; and

- where the buyer has become insolvent.

Exercise of this right can be effective as a means of enforcing payment. However, the right cannot be exercised if the seller has already made delivery, since one cannot retain possession if one no longer has it!

Stoppage in transit – s 44 of the Sale of Goods Act 1979

This is a right of the unpaid seller to resume possession of the goods if they are still in transit (that is, with an independent carrier). The right can be exercised only if the buyer has become insolvent. This right is in fact seldom used and is exercised by the seller contacting the carrier and requiring the carrier not to deliver the goods to the buyer but to restore them to the seller. The seller must pay the cost of this.

Resale – s 48 of the Sale of Goods Act 1979

An unpaid seller who still has the goods (or recovers them by stoppage in transit) may be able to resell the goods. The unpaid seller can do this in the following circumstances:

- the goods are perishable and the seller gives notice to the buyer of his intention to resell them and the buyer does not within a reasonable time pay or tender the price;

- the seller has expressly reserved the right of resale on the buyer making default.

Where the seller exercises this right, he sells as owner and, thus, if he resells the goods for more than the buyer had agreed to pay, the seller makes an additional profit which he is entitled to keep. He must, of course, refund to the buyer any part of the price paid by the buyer except to the extent that doing so would leave the seller making a loss.

f the seller makes a loss on the resale, he is entitled to claim
that loss as damages from the buyer.

Of course, in addition to the rights of resale under s 48, the
seller is entitled to resell the goods if the buyer has repudiated
the contract and the seller has accepted that repudiation.

11 Buyer's remedies

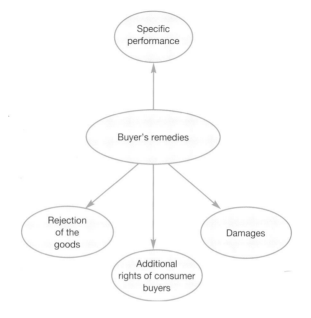

Specific performance – s 52 of the Sale of Goods Act 1979

This is an order of the court directed to the seller to carry out the contract, that is, to deliver the goods, and is available only in restricted circumstances:

- the seller's breach must be breach of a duty to deliver specific or ascertained goods; and

- the situation must be one where an award of damages would not be an adequate remedy. This is likely to be the case only where the goods are unique or virtually unique.

Rejection of the goods

The buyer has the right to reject goods for breach of condition. This right and the restrictions upon it were explained on p 53.

When the buyer is entitled to and does reject the goods, he is entitled to recover any of the price already paid. In addition to rejecting the goods, and irrespective of whether repayment of the price is claimed, the buyer may bring a claim for damages for:

- storage expenses if any; and
- non-delivery.

Damages

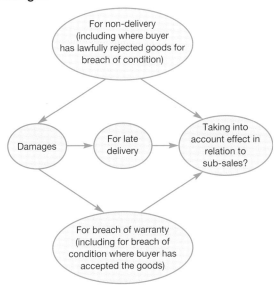

Damages for non-delivery

It is assumed that the buyer goes on to the market and buys replacement goods immediately on the day the seller should have delivered and failed to do so.

● Thus, the *prima facie* measure of damages is X–Y, where:
  X = the market price on the date when the seller should have delivered the goods; and
  Y = the contract price.

● Thus, if the contract price exceeds the market price on that date, the *prima facie* measure of damages is zero and the buyer is entitled only to nominal damages.

● If the buyer chooses not to buy replacement goods immediately, then that is normally irrelevant and the buyer takes the risk of the price subsequently rising and takes the benefit if the price subsequently falls.

● Normally, it is also equally irrelevant that the buyer may have made greater or lesser losses because of the existence of sub-sales made. It is assumed that the buyer will have bought replacement goods in the market in order to fulfil any sub-contracts he may happen to have.

● However, the buyer's losses in connection with sub-sale will be taken into account where the buyer's contract with the seller contemplated sub-sales of the very same goods and where the sub-sale contract was for the sale of the very same goods that the seller was supposed to supply to the buyer. In this situation, the buyer is therefore likely to recover more than the *prima facie* measure (*Re Hall and Pims Arbitration* (1928)).

Damages for late delivery

Late delivery is usually a breach of condition. Where the buyer rejects the goods, the measure of damages is as for non-delivery. Where the buyer accepts the goods after late delivery, the buyer will usually be awarded X–Y, where:

X = the market price on the date on which the goods should have been delivered; and

Y = the market price on the date on which the goods are actually delivered.

Thus, if the market value on the later date is higher, the buyer's loss is zero.

If the amount of the buyer's loss is affected because of possible sub-sales, this will be taken into account to adjust the loss up or down. For example, the market value of the goods may have dropped, but the buyer may have suffered no loss because he was able to use the goods, despite their delayed delivery to himself, to fulfil a contract he was obliged to fulfil anyway (*Wertheim v Chicoutimi Pulp* (1911)).

Damages for breach of warranty – s 53 of the Sale of Goods Act 1979

The typical breach is a breach of an express term of the contract or a breach of the implied conditions as to satisfactory quality. Where the buyer has accepted the goods, damages for breach of condition are assessed in the same way as for breach of warranty.

The *prima facie* measure of damages is X–Y, where:

X = the value the goods would have had if they had complied with the contract; and

Y = the value the goods actually had on delivery.

Again, however, if the buyer has, despite the breach of contract and, without any loss to himself, been able to use the goods to fulfil sub-contracts made, then the buyer is not entitled to the prima facie measure of damages. This is because, in that situation, the buyer has suffered no loss (*Bence Graphics International Ltd v Fasson UK* (1996)).

Where the buyer has suffered consequential loss, then that loss can be claimed. For example, the goods supplied may have injured the buyer or damaged his other property.

Lack of conformity with the contract

Part 5A of the Sale of Goods Act 1979 sets out *additional* rights of buyers in consumer cases. These rights *do not replace* the rights set out in ss 13-15 of the Act. The new rights apply if (a) the buyer is a consumer, and (b) the goods do not conform to the contract at the time of delivery. The definition of a consumer is the one set out in the Unfair Contract Terms Act 1977 (see p 66.) Goods do not conform to the contract if there is breach of an express term of the contract or a breach of one of the terms implied by ss 13-15 of the Act (s 48F of the Sale of Goods Act 1979). If the goods do not conform to the contract at any time within six months of the date of delivery, there is a (rebuttable) presumption that they did not conform at the date of delivery. This presumption does not apply if it is incompatible with the nature of the goods or the nature of the lack of conformity.

Hierarchy of rights

If the goods bought do not conform to the contract the consumer is given a hierarchy of rights: first, to require the seller to repair or replace the goods; second, to require the seller to reduce the price by an appropriate amount or to rescind the contract.

Repair or replacement must be achieved within a reasonable time and the cost or repairing or replacing must be borne by the seller. Although repair or replacement are the primary remedies, the buyer cannot require the seller to repair or replace the goods where it would be impossible for the seller to do so, or where the remedy sought would be disproportionate in relation to another remedy. Where the buyer does require the seller to repair or replace the goods, he must not reject the goods and terminate the contract until the seller has been given a reasonable time to repair or replace the goods.

repair or replacement is disproportionate, or is not achieved by the seller within a reasonable time of being requested, or cannot be achieved without significant inconvenience to the buyer, the buyer is entitled to a reduction of the price (by an appropriate amount) or rescission of the contract. However, if the buyer does rescind, any reimbursement to the buyer may be reduced to take account of any use of the goods which he has had.

Other statutes

The Supply of Goods (Implied Terms) Act 1973 and the Supply of Goods and Services Act 1982 have been amended so that virtually identical rights are included where goods supplied to a consumer do not conform to the contract.

12 Agency

Nature of agency

An agent has authority to make contracts with third parties on behalf of another person, the principal. Having made the contracts the agent usually drops out of the picture and the contracts take effect between the principal and the third parties. Only an agent with some type of authority to act for the principal has the right to make a contract which binds the principal. (However, in Chapter 4 we saw that a person who is not an agent sometimes has the *power*, but not the *right*, to pass a good title to another person's goods.)

Creation of agency

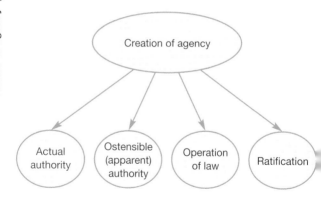

Actual authority

An agent may be given actual authority either expressly or impliedly. Actual authority arises where the principal and agent agree, expressly or impliedly, that the agent should have authority.

Express actual authority

An agency may be created by the principal giving express instructions, for example, where a seller puts goods into an auction sale asking for them to be sold.

Implied actual authority

This arises where the principal agrees with the agent that the agent should have the authority but does so other than by express words. For example, it would apply if the principal appoints someone to a certain position, for example, store manager, or company managing director. In that case, and in the absence of any express statement to the contrary, the principal will be taken to have agreed with the appointee that he should enter, on the principal's behalf, all the types of transaction which someone in the appointee's position would usually have authority to enter. Thus, someone who is, say, a managing director will automatically have all the usual authority given to someone in that position, unless the principal has expressly placed a restriction on it (*Hely-Hutchinson v Brayhead* (1968)).

Ostensible (apparent) authority

The doctrine of ostensible authority is based on estoppel (*Freeman and Lockyer v Buckhurst Park Properties* (1964)). The idea is that if the principal has held out the agent as having authority, it would not normally be right to allow the principal subsequently to deny that the agent did have that authority. The requirements for the doctrine to apply are:

- the principal made a representation that the agent had authority to enter the transaction;

- the representation was intended to be acted and relied upon by the other party to the contract (the third party);

- the representation was relied upon by the third party.

Where these three requirements are fulfilled, the principal is estopped as against the third party from denying that the agent had authority.

Apparent authority becomes important where the agent is appointed to a recognised position, but is expressly told not to make certain types of contract which someone in that position would normally have the authority to make. The principal, by appointing the agent to the position in question, has thereby represented to the world at large that the agent has all the usual authority that goes with that position. A third party, who does not know of the express restriction on that usual authority, may well enter the contract assuming that the agent has the full usual authority of someone in that particular position. In *Panorama Developments v Fidelis Furnishing Fabrics* (1971), a company secretary made a number of contracts over a period of time ordering minicabs to collect and take people to and from the airport. He was in fact making these contracts to convey relatives or friends of his, but was ordering the cars in the name of his company. It was held that the company was liable to pay for the cabs because the making of such contracts was within the usual authority of a company secretary.

It is important to remember that apparent authority gives a third party a right to enforce the contract made by the agent against the principal but does not give the principal the right to enforce the contract. Also, a third party who knows or ought to know that the agent had no actual authority cannot claim that the agent had apparent authority.

Watteau v Fenwick

In *Watteau v Fenwick* (1893), the manager of a pub was forbidden by the owner to buy tobacco on credit. In contravention of these instructions, the manager (the agent) did buy tobacco on credit. The salesman thought that the agent owned the pub. It was held that the agent had authority and that the principal was bound. The agent did not have actual uthority because he had been forbidden to make the urchase. He also could not have apparent authority because he salesman could not claim that a principal of whom he was unaware had made a representation to him. It was held that the agent had 'usual authority'. However, the precise way in which he agent's authority arose is unclear and some have doubted whether the case would now be followed. Also, it is important o realise that the term 'usual authority' can have other meanings. Usual authority can be a species of actual authority because the principal and agent have agreed that an agent appointed to a position has the authority which usually goes with such a position) or a species of apparent authority (because by appointing an agent to a position, the principal represents to third parties that the agent has the authority which usually goes with such a position).

Operation of law

Agency is usually something that is agreed between the principal and agent (actual authority) or arises by virtue of the principal having represented the agent as having authority (ostensible authority). However, sometimes, the law imposes an agency relationship.

Agency of necessity

This arises where three conditions are all satisfied:

- there is an actual commercial necessity for the agency;
- it is impossible for the 'agent' to get the principal's instructions;
- the 'agent' acts *bona fide* in the interests of all parties.

The occurrence of these requirements was more common years ago than now, because communications are now so much better. Years ago, a carrier of a cargo which suddenly started to ferment whilst in the Middle East could not easily contact the cargo's owner back in England before deciding that he really had to sell the cargo there and then before it became useless. Nowadays, the facilities of telephones and fax machines make the 'necessity' for the carrier to sell the cargo without first getting the owner's authority much less likely to arise.

Statutory agency

Sometimes statute imposes an agency. Thus, for example, in the case of credit agreements which are regulated by the Consumer Credit Act 1974 and where there is a business connection between the creditor (finance house) and the dealer (retailer), the latter is made agent of the former in carrying out 'antecedent negotiations' (s 56 of the Consumer Credit Act 1956 – see p 148).

Ratification

Where someone purports to act as agent, but does not have actual or apparent authority for his acts, the 'principal' will not be bound by the acts in question unless the principal subsequently ratifies them. If he does ratify them, the ratification is retrospective and relates back to when the acts were carried out. Ratification therefore retrospectively creates actual authority. A contract can be ratified, however, only if the following conditions are all satisfied:

- the 'agent' must have purported to act as agent. Ratification will therefore not be possible where the agent has acted as if for himself, that is, without disclosing that he was acting for someone else (*Keighley, Maxsted and Co v Durant* (1901));

- the principal must have been in existence at the time the contract was made;

- the principal must, at the time it was made, have had contractual capacity to make the contract;

- the principal must have been named, or ascertainable, when the contract was made;

- at the time of ratification, the principal either must have full knowledge of the material facts, or else must have the intention to ratify whatever may be the facts;

- the principal must ratify within the stated time limit, if any, or else within a reasonable time.

Relationships created by the agency

Disclosed agency

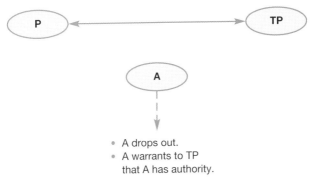

- A drops out.
- A warrants to TP that A has authority.

Where the agent discloses at the time the contract is made that he is acting as agent, two consequences generally flow:

- unless otherwise agreed, the agent gives to the third party a *warranty of authority*. This enables the third party to maintain an action for damages against the agent if it turns out that the 'agent' had no authority to make the contract;

- apart from the warranty of authority, the agent drops out of the picture and is not liable on the contract.

These rules apply when the fact of the agency is disclosed to the third party, irrespective of whether the particular principal is identified.

Undisclosed agency

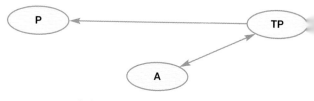

- A does not drop out.
- TP can sue either A or P on the contract.
- If P sues TP, TP can rely on defences available to TP if sued by A.

Where the agent fails to disclose at the time the contract is made that he is acting as agent, the third party can hold the agent liable as if he were the principal. In fact, the third party has an option whereby the third party can hold either the principal liable or the agent liable as if he were the principal.

Should the principal seek to hold the third party liable, this is generally permitted. In that case, however, any set-off or defence available to the third party against the agent before the third party discovered the existence of the principal can be relied upon by the third party against the principal.

The principal is not allowed, however, to hold the third party liable in the following circumstances:

- if it is contrary to the terms of the contract;
- if the identity of the principal is a significant factor (*Said v Butt* (1920)).

Agent's duties to principal

These are:

- to exercise due care and diligence in the performance of his duties;

- to render an account when so required;

- not to allow duty and interest to conflict. This includes:
  - not, without disclosing it to the principal, to become a principal as against his principal (*Armstrong v Jackson* (1917));
  - not to make secret profit from his position;

- not, without permission, to delegate his authority;

- not, without permission, to disclose or make use of confidential information obtained in his role as agent.

Principal's duties to agent

These are:

- to pay remuneration and/or commission as and when due according to the terms of their agreement;

- to indemnify the agent for acts lawfully done and liabilities properly incurred in the course of carrying out the agency.

Termination of agency

Termination by principal

As a general rule, the principal can withdraw the agent's authority at any time. This is subject, however, to the doctrine of ostensible authority, whereby a third party who is unaware of the principal's withdrawal of authority may nevertheless be able to hold the principal liable.

Termination by operation of law

An agency is normally terminated by the occurrence of any of the following events:

- death of the principal;

- bankruptcy of the principal;

- principal becoming mentally incapable;

- principal becoming an enemy of the country.

Specialist agents

There are particular rules applicable to particular types of agent such as auctioneers, estate agents, *del credere* agents and mercantile agents.

Commercial agents

The Commercial Agents (Council Directive) Regulations 1993 apply to independent commercial agents who have continuing authority to negotiate the sale or purchase of goods. They do not apply to agents who are employees, company directors or partners. In relation to those agents to whom they apply, these regulations supplement or vary the position at common law. Their effect includes the following:

- The agent and the principal are each under a duty to the other to act dutifully and in good faith and have various other specific duties, such as the agent's duty to provide the principal with all necessary information available to the agent.

- The agent has a general right to reasonable remuneration for work done.

- There is a minimum period of notice for termination of the agency and there are provisions for the agent to receive compensation when the agreement is terminated. The notion is that where the regulations apply, broadly where the agent has authority to buy and sell on the principal's behalf, the agent will have an interest in the business which his activities will have helped to build up. Upon termination, he is therefore entitled to compensation.

13 International sales

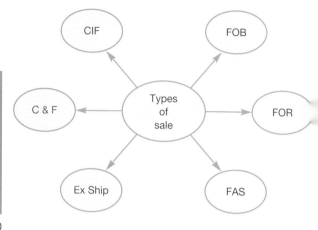

FOB contracts

Different contracts may contain different provisions. However, the *Free On Board* (FOB) contract is one which has come traditionally to have certain features and, if these are not expressly spelt out and are not contradicted in the written contract, they will normally be assumed to be present in a contract which is termed FOB.

The classic features are as follows:

- The buyer arranges carriage of the goods in whatever ship the buyer chooses. Thus, the buyer incurs the cost of freight on the ship and insurance of the goods from the moment they are loaded.

- The buyer will nominate the ship. If there is a contract stipulation for this to be done by a certain date, then failure to nominate the ship by that date will be a breach of condition by the buyer (*Bunge Corporation v Tradax* (1981)).

The seller's duty is to convey the goods to the ship and have them loaded.

Property in the goods will pass when the parties intend it to, and their intention will normally be that property is to pass when the goods are loaded onto the ship. If the buyer fails to nominate a ship, the seller cannot load. Thus, property cannot pass. In that case, unless the price was payable on a day certain, the seller will not be able to sue for the price, but will be confined to a claim for damages for non-acceptance (*Colley v Overseas Exporters* (1921)).

Similarly, risk will normally pass, according to the parties' intention, as the goods pass over the ship's rail. The seller is under a duty to give the buyer notice of shipment, to enable the buyer to insure the goods. Failure to give notice will leave the goods at the seller's risk.

Individual contracts may vary one or more of the classic terms, for example, to provide that the seller undertakes to arrange carriage by sea and/or insurance.

CIF contracts

In a *Cost, Insurance, Freight* (CIF) contract, the cost includes insurance and freight. Thus, it is for the seller to arrange the carriage of the goods by sea to the destination port specified in the contract. It is also for the seller to arrange the insurance of the goods during the voyage. The key feature of a CIF contract is that it focuses on the delivery of documents and payment against delivery of those documents. The usual documents to be provided by the seller are:

- A bill of lading, which represents the contract for the carriage of the goods by sea.

- An insurance policy, which represents the contract of marine insurance.

- An invoice, which asks for payment of the price. If payment is to be made by the buyer accepting a bill of exchange, the the bill of exchange will accompany the documents so that the buyer, upon receipt of the documents, can 'accept' the bill of exchange and return it to the seller.

In a CIF contract, the buyer has two rights of rejection:

- Reject the documents if they do not conform to the contract (for example, if the bill of lading shows that the goods were loaded onto the vessel after the date specified in the contract). If the buyer fails to reject the documents when he knows they are not in order, he will be estopped from rejecting them later (*Panchaud Frères v Etablissement General Grain* (1970)). Assuming that the documents are in order, the buyer has no right to reject the documents even if he can prove that the goods are non-conforming. In that situation, he must pay against the documents and may later reject the goods upon their arrival and then claim back the price (*Gill and Dufus v Berger* (1984)).

- Reject the goods, upon their arrival, if they do not conform to the contract (*Kwei Tek Chao v British Traders and Shippers Ltd* (1954)).

Assuming the goods have become ascertained, property passes to the buyer at the time the documents are taken up. If the buyer subsequently exercises his right to reject the goods, property will revert to the seller. If the goods are not ascertained but are a specified quantity from an identified bulk, then the buyer will acquire a property right consisting of an undivided share in the bulk (see p 8).

Risk, however, will normally be intended to pass to the buyer upon shipment even if the goods were already afloat when the contract was made. The buyer does, however, have the benefit of the insurance policy transferred to him retrospectively from the date of shipment.

Other types of sale contract

Ex Works

The buyer is to collect the goods from the seller's premises.

FOR or FOT

Free On Rail, or *Free On Train*, is a term used to describe a contract where the seller will deliver the goods to the rail and arrange their loading onto the wagons.

FAS

A *Free Along Side* contract is similar to an FOB except that the seller undertakes to leave the goods alongside a ship (usually a ship to be nominated by the buyer) rather than undertaking to have them loaded onto the ship.

C & F

A *Cost and Freight* contract is similar to a CIF contract except that the seller does not undertake to arrange insurance.

Ex Ship

This is similar to a CIF contract except that the seller's duty goes further. The seller undertakes to get the goods to the port of destination and make them available to be delivered to the buyer from the ship at that port. The seller retains the risk until arrival at that port.

Payment arrangements

Traditional method

The buyer is sent the shipping documents (bill of lading and insurance policy) together with a bill of exchange. The buyer 'accepts' the bill (assuming that the bill provides for payment at a later date) and returns it to the seller. The seller then has a bill of exchange which is a negotiable instrument which can be indorsed (for example, to a bank) in return for immediate payment. The indorsee (the bank) can retain the bill until the due date for payment when the indorsee is entitled to payment from the 'acceptor', that is, the buyer. In practice, the documents will be sent by the seller via the international banking system to a bank in the buyer's country, that bank having authority, if the shipping documents are in order, to accept or pay the bill on the buyer's behalf.

International letter of credit

The contract may require the buyer to open a letter of credit. This is a device to give the seller some added assurance that he will be paid. The buyer instructs a bank in his country (the issuing bank) to open a credit with a bank in the seller's country (the advising bank). This authorises the advising bank to pay the price (or accept the bill of exchange) on presentation of the shipping documents to the advising bank. The type of credit to be opened depends upon the terms of the contract.

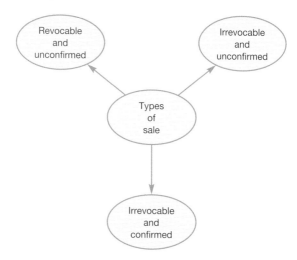

Revocable and unconfirmed

Neither the issuing nor advising bank enters into a commitment to the seller. If payment is not made, the seller can look only to the buyer for a remedy.

Irrevocable and unconfirmed

The issuing bank enters into a legally binding commitment to the seller that it will pay according to the terms of the credit, that is, if conforming documents are presented before expiry of the credit.

Irrevocable and confirmed

Both the issuing bank and the advising bank enter legally binding commitments to the seller.

In the case of an irrevocable letter of credit, the issuing bank cannot refuse to pay just because the goods themselves are proven to be non-conforming. The bank's duty is to pay against conforming documents. (The same is true of the advising bank if it has confirmed the credit.) The buyer is then under a duty to indemnify the bank for its payment. A buyer who wishes to protect himself against the risk of thus having paid for goods which then prove to be non-conforming may, as part of the contract, require the seller to provide a performance guarantee via the international banking system.

International sales

Payment arrangements

14 Consumer credit – categories of agreement

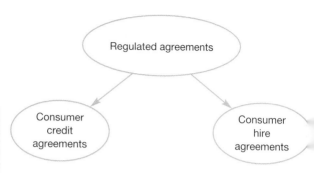

The Consumer Credit Act 1974 regulates regulated agreements, unless they are 'exempt' agreements. In addition, the Act contains definitions of various sub-categories of agreement, including:

- debtor–creditor–supplier agreements;
- debtor–creditor agreements;
- restricted-use credit agreements;
- unrestricted-use credit agreements;
- small agreements;
- non-commercial agreements.

Regulated consumer credit agreement (s 8 of the Consumer Credit Act 1974)

See flow chart on facing page.

Box 1

'Credit' includes a cash loan and any other form of financial accommodation (s 9(1) of the Consumer Credit Act 1974). Hire purchase is a form of credit. Simple hire is not a form of credit. However, a hire agreement can be a regulated agreement if it is a consumer hire agreement (see flow chart on p 121).

Flow chart to determine if agreement is a regulated consumer credit agreement

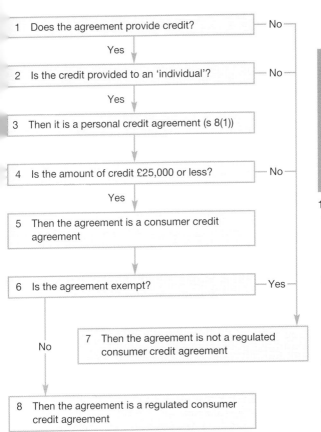

Box 2

A partnership is an individual. However, a company or other corporate body is not. Thus, an agreement for a loan or other form of credit to a company cannot be a regulated agreement.

Box 3

Personal credit agreements are not regulated by the Act unless the amount of credit is £25,000 or less and the agreement is not exempt. However, personal credit agreements which are not regulated are nevertheless subject to one set of provisions in the Consumer Credit Act 1974; they are the extortionate credit bargain provisions in ss 137–40.

Box 4

In the case of a 'running-account' credit agreement, the significant figure is the credit limit. If that is £25,000 or less, this question is to be answered 'Yes'. In the case of 'fixed-sum' credit, the significant figure is the amount agreed to be advanced and this amount does not include the cost of the credit – that is, it does not include the interest or any other amount which falls within the 'total charge for credit' (see p 126).

Boxes 5 and 6

A consumer credit agreement is regulated only if it is not an exempt agreement. For 'exempt agreements', see p 123.

Regulated consumer hire agreement (s 15 of the Consumer Credit Act 1974)

See flow chart on facing page.

Box 2

A partnership is an individual. However, a company or other corporate body is not. Thus, for example, an agreement whereby a company hires a photocopier cannot be a regulated agreement.

Flow chart to determine if agreement is a regulated consumer hire agreement

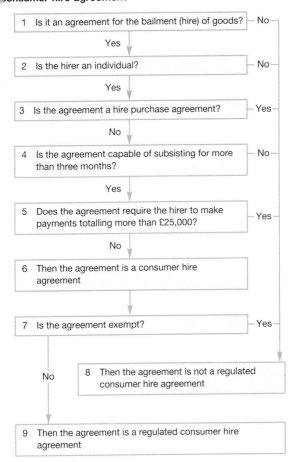

1 Is it an agreement for the bailment (hire) of goods? — No

Yes ↓

2 Is the hirer an individual? — No

Yes ↓

3 Is the agreement a hire purchase agreement? — Yes

No ↓

4 Is the agreement capable of subsisting for more than three months? — No

Yes ↓

5 Does the agreement require the hirer to make payments totalling more than £25,000? — Yes

No ↓

6 Then the agreement is a consumer hire agreement

↓

7 Is the agreement exempt? — Yes

No ↓

8 Then the agreement is not a regulated consumer hire agreement

9 Then the agreement is a regulated consumer hire agreement

Consumer credit I

121

Regulated consumer hire agreement

Box 3

A hire purchase agreement cannot be a consumer hire agreement. However, it can be a consumer credit agreement (see flow chart on p 119).

Box 4

Short term hirings of three months or less are not caught by the Act. If, however, a three month hire agreement contains a clause enabling the parties to renew the agreement, it will be *capable* of subsisting for more than three months.

Box 5

What is looked at here is not the amount of each instalment of rental, but the total amount which is required to be paid by the hirer under the agreement. If the agreement contains a clause entitling the hirer to terminate the agreement after, say, five months, then the total amount which the agreement requires the hirer to pay will include only those amounts which the hirer will have to pay if the hirer terminates the agreement at the first opportunity, that is, after five months.

Box 7

The only type of consumer hire agreement which can fall within the exempt category is where the agreement is for the hire of a gas, water or electricity meter.

See diagram on facing page.

Note

The low cost credit exemption applies only where debtor–creditor credit is offered on a limited basis to a particular class or classes of individuals and where the APR does not exceed a benchmark rate. That benchmark rate is: (i) in the case of credit provided by a credit union, 12.7%; and (ii) in other cases, 1% higher than the highest of the base rates of the major UK banks. Where the APR under the agreement cannot be increased, the benchmark rate is that applicable 28 days before the agreement was made. Where the APR can be varied, the agreement is low cost if the APR cannot at any time exceed the benchmark rate applicable 28 days earlier.

House purchase mortgage loans from local authority or named bank, building society, insurance company, etc.

Fixed-sum, debtor–creditor–supplier agreement where credit to be repaid within a year in no more than four instalments

Exempt agreements

Running-account debtor–creditor–supplier agreement where each periodical account to be paid in a single payment

Debtor–creditor–supplier agreement financing purchase of land where number of payments is four or fewer

Credit to be used in connection with overseas trade

Low cost, debtor–creditor agreement

Hire of gas, water or electricity meter

Debtor–creditor–supplier and debtor–creditor agreements (s 12 of the Consumer Credit Act 1974)

This definition aims to identify credit agreements where *either*:

- the credit is to enable the debtor to buy goods or services from the creditor (that is, the creditor is the same person as the supplier of the goods or services); *or*

- the credit is to enable the debtor to buy goods or services supplied by one person and the credit is provided by a creditor under 'arrangements' between the creditor and the supplier.

Thus, in a debtor–creditor–supplier agreement, either the creditor and the supplier will be one and the same person, or there will be arrangements, a business connection, between them. The arrangements will be arrangements whereby the creditor is prepared to provide credit to customers of the supplier. A credit agreement which is not a debtor–creditor–supplier agreement is a debtor–creditor agreement.

Restricted-use credit and unrestricted-use credit (s 11 of the Consumer Credit Act 1974)

Credit provided in such a way that the debtor is free to use it as he chooses is unrestricted-use credit. If it is not provided in that way, then it may be restricted-use. Typical examples of restricted-use credit are hire purchase, conditional sale and credit sale agreements.

Small agreements (s 17 of the Consumer Credit Act 1974)

- A *fixed-sum* credit agreement is a small agreement if the amount of credit (ignoring charge for the credit) is £50 or less.

- A *running-account* credit agreement is a small agreement if the credit limit does not exceed £50.

inked transactions (s 19 of the Consumer redit Act 1974)

ow chart to determine if a transaction is a linked ansaction

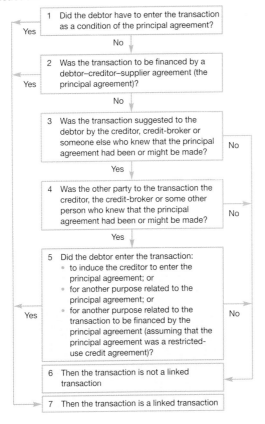

The total charge for credit

Add up the interest and other charges payable under the following transactions

- The credit agreement +

- Transactions entered into in compliance with the credit agreement +

- Transactions required to be made or maintained as a condition of the making of the credit agreement +

- Transactions for the provision of security +

- Any credit-brokerage contract relating to the credit agreement.

Subtract from the above sum the following charges

- Default charges.

- Charges that would be equally payable by a customer paying cash.

- Variable bank charges on current accounts, charges for care maintenance or protection of goods or land (provided the debtor has a free choice as to from where he gets these services or, alternatively, if the charges are payable only in the event of something going wrong).

- Club membership charges which entitle the member to other benefits apart from credit facilities.

- Motor insurance premiums.

- Other insurance premiums (that is, if the insurance was optional for the debtor, or if he had a free choice as to which insurer to use, or if the policy monies are to be used to repay the credit).

15 Consumer credit – triangular transactions

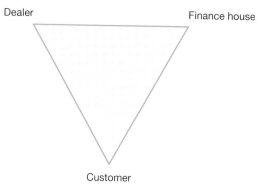

Dealer   Finance house

Customer

We are here dealing with the situation where a dealer has an arrangement with a bank or finance company ('the finance house'), whereby the latter is in principle prepared to finance the dealer's customers so that they can acquire the dealer's goods. It may be that the finance house makes a loan agreement with the customer, thereby lending money to the customer, enabling the customer to buy the goods. Equally, it could be that the finance house buys the goods from the dealer and then contracts with the customer to supply those same goods to the customer on credit or hire terms. The following table indicates the possible combinations, where FH = finance house.

- The table applies irrespective of whether the agreement is a regulated agreement.

- In those cases where the finance house is supplier of the goods to the customer, if the customer has a complaint on the ground of a breach of contract, for example, that the goods are not of satisfactory quality or fit for their purpose, it is the finance house against whom the customer must bring proceedings. The customer will be able to proceed against the dealer only if he can establish a collateral contract or, possibly, negligence (*Andrews v Hopkinson* (1956)).

Type of agreement between FH and customer	Does FH buy the goods from the dealer?	FH owner of the goods?	Is FH supplier of the goods to the customer?	When will the customer become owner of the goods?
Hire purchase	Yes	Yes (until customer completes hp payments to FH) and exercises option to purchase	Yes	When he completes hp payments to FH and exercises option to purchase
Cond- itional sale	Yes	Yes (until customer completes payments to FH under conditional sale agree- ment)	Yes	When he completes payments to FH under conditional sale agreement
Credit sale	Yes	FH acquires ownership by purchase from dealer, but passes ownership to buyer	Yes	Before or at the time of delivery of goods to customer: see Sale of Goods Act rules on passing of property
Simple hire	Yes	Yes	Yes	Never
Loan	No	No	No	Before or at the time of delivery of goods to customer: see Sale of Goods Act rules on passing of property

Agency of the dealer

- At common law, the dealer is not the agent of the finance house in any of the above situations (*Branwhite v Worcester Works Finance* (1969)).

- Where, however, the agreements are regulated agreements, the dealer can be the agent of the finance house during antecedent negotiations (s 56 of the Consumer Credit Act 1974). This statutory agency does not, however, apply where the agreement is a consumer hire agreement. The statutory agency most commonly applies where goods are bought with a credit card, or with a loan arranged by the dealer, or under a triangular hire purchase transaction.

- The statutory agency means that the finance house is liable for statements and promises made by the dealer to the customer during antecedent negotiations, provided those statements or promises relate to the transaction being financed. Suppose that the transaction is the acquisition of a car by the customer and that it involves the customer trading in a car in part-exchange. It may be that the dealer agrees a part-exchange allowance and undertakes that, out of that part-exchange allowance, he will pay off the customer's existing hire purchase debt on the car the customer is trading in. If so, that promise is one for which the finance house can be held liable (*Forthright Finance Ltd v Ingate* (1997)). Alternatively, if the dealer described a car as suitable for towing a caravan and it turned out not to be suitable, the finance house would be liable for the dealer's statement.

16 Consumer credit – trading control

Licensing

The licensing system is run by the Office of Fair Trading (OFT).

Anyone carrying on a business in one or more of the following categories needs a licence covering that category.

Categories C, D, E and F are collectively termed ancillary credit businesses. Carrying on a business in any of the categories without a licence covering that category is unlicensed trading. Even if the category is covered by a licence, canvassing off

ade premises amounts to unlicensed trading unless
nvassing off trade premises is expressly authorised by the
ence.

anctions for unlicensed trading are twofold:

Unlicensed trading is a criminal offence (s 39 of the
Consumer Credit Act 1974).

An agreement may be unenforceable if made by an
unlicensed trader:

– a regulated agreement is unenforceable by the creditor
  or owner if he was not appropriately licensed when the
  agreement was made (s 40 of the Consumer Credit
  Act 1974);

– an ancillary credit agreement is unenforceable by the
  trader (credit-broker, debt counsellor, debt collector,
  etc) if the trader was not appropriately licensed when
  the agreement was made (s 148 of the Consumer Credit
  Act 1974);

– a regulated agreement is unenforceable if it was
  made following an introduction by a credit-broker
  who was not appropriately licensed at the time the
  introduction was made (s 149 of the Consumer
  Credit Act 1974);

– the trader can, however, ask the OFT for a validating
  order enabling the trader to enforce one or more
  agreements which would otherwise be unenforceable
  under the above rules.

Canvassing

The flow chart on p 134 covers the definition of canvassing off
trade premises (in s 48 of the Consumer Credit Act 1974) and
sets out the legal controls on this activity. Canvassing is used to
persuade individuals to enter into regulated agreements.

Flow chart to determine if a salesperson was canvassing a regulated agreement off trade premises

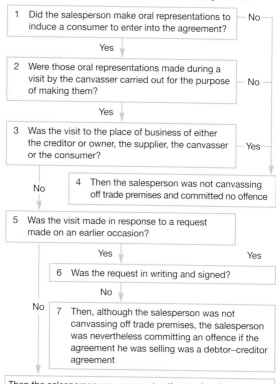

1 Did the salesperson make oral representations to induce a consumer to enter into the agreement? — No

Yes ↓

2 Were those oral representations made during a visit by the canvasser carried out for the purpose of making them? — No

Yes ↓

3 Was the visit to the place of business of either the creditor or owner, the supplier, the canvasser or the consumer? — Yes

No

4 Then the salesperson was not canvassing off trade premises and committed no offence

5 Was the visit made in response to a request made on an earlier occasion?

Yes ↓   Yes

6 Was the request in writing and signed?

No ↓

No

7 Then, although the salesperson was not canvassing off trade premises, the salesperson was nevertheless committing an offence if the agreement he was selling was a debtor–creditor agreement

Then the salesperson was canvassing the regulated agreement off trade premises. If the agreement was a debtor–creditor agreement, the canvasser was committing a criminal offence. If it was a consumer hire agreement or a debtor–creditor–supplier agreement, the canvasser should have been operating under a licence specifically permitting such canvassing

Door to door selling

This method of selling of loans is controlled by the Act. It protects people of limited means from being persuaded by creditors to take loans at extortionate rates of interest. To canvass debtor–creditor credit 'off trade premises' is an offence under s 49(1) of the Consumer Credit Act 1974. See flow chart on facing page.

Canvassing – summary

Canvassing off trade premises is controlled in two ways:

- it is an offence to canvass debtor–creditor agreements off trade premises (s 49 of the Consumer Credit Act 1974);

- the canvassing of other regulated agreements (debtor–creditor–supplier agreements and consumer hire agreements) is permitted provided the canvasser is operating under a licence which expressly authorises such canvassing.

Other criminal offences

- Sending out *circulars to minors* inviting them to obtain credit or goods on hire (s 50 of the Consumer Credit Act 1974).

- Sending out an *unsolicited credit token*, other than a renewal one (s 51 of the Consumer Credit Act 1974).

- Putting out a credit or hire *advertisement* which in a material respect is *misleading* (s 46 of the Consumer Credit Act 1974).

- Putting out a credit or hire *advertisement* which infringes the Consumer Credit (Advertisements) Regulations 2004. These regulations set out detailed requirements as to the contents of advertisements controlled by the Consumer Credit Act 1974. They also brought in the idea of a 'typical APR' below which the creditor expects to do 66% of the business to which the advertisement relates.

Note that the Consumer Credit (Quotations) Regulations 1989, which laid down the required form of quotations, were repealed in 1997.

17 Consumer credit – documentation and cancellation

Agreements subject to the documentation requirements

Flow chart to determine whether the documentation provisions of the Consumer Credit Act 1974 apply to the agreement

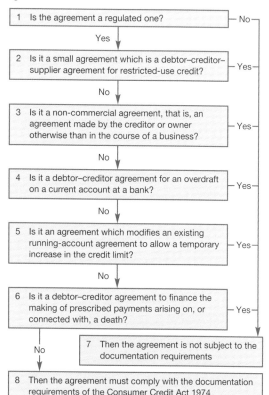

1. Is the agreement a regulated one? — No
   Yes ↓
2. Is it a small agreement which is a debtor–creditor–supplier agreement for restricted-use credit? — Yes
   No ↓
3. Is it a non-commercial agreement, that is, an agreement made by the creditor or owner otherwise than in the course of a business? — Yes
   No ↓
4. Is it a debtor–creditor agreement for an overdraft on a current account at a bank? — Yes
   No ↓
5. Is it an agreement which modifies an existing running-account agreement to allow a temporary increase in the credit limit? — Yes
   No ↓
6. Is it a debtor–creditor agreement to finance the making of prescribed payments arising on, or connected with, a death? — Yes
   No ↓
7. Then the agreement is not subject to the documentation requirements
8. Then the agreement must comply with the documentation requirements of the Consumer Credit Act 1974

he agreements in Boxes 2–6 are exempted by s 74 of the
onsumer Credit Act 1974 from having to comply with the
ocumentation requirements.

he documentation requirements

Content of the written agreement

he Consumer Credit (Agreements) Regulations 1983 made
nder s 60 of the Consumer Credit Act 1974 require the
greement to include (*inter alia*):

- the amount of credit or the credit limit;
- the amounts and timings of payments;
- the total charge for credit;
- the APR (annual percentage rate of the total charge for
  credit);
- details of any security provided by the debtor or hirer; and
- information on legal protections for the consumer as to
  rights of cancellation, termination, repossession of goods,
  etc.

Form of the agreement

- The agreement must be legible and it must embody all
  its terms (other than implied terms) at the time when the
  debtor or hirer signs it (s 61 of the Consumer Credit Act
  1974).
- The agreement must have the appropriate heading, as stated
  by the Consumer Credit (Agreements) Regulations, for
  example, 'Hire Purchase Agreement Regulated by the
  Consumer Credit Act 1974'.
- The statements about various protections for the debtor or
  hirer must be in the form required by the regulations.
- The agreement must contain a signature box.

Signatures

The agreement must be signed by the debtor or hirer and by, o on behalf of, the creditor or owner (s 61 of the Consumer Credi Act 1974).

Copies (ss 62 and 63 of the Consumer Credit Act 1974)

- If the agreement is made on the occasion when the debtor o hirer signs it, he must be given a copy of the executed agreement there and then. The agreement is executed when it is signed by both parties.

- If the agreement is not made on the occasion when the debtor or hirer signs, there arises a requirement for him to be given two copies:

  - on the occasion when he signs, he must be given a copy of the unexecuted agreement; and

  - within seven days of the making of the agreement, he must receive a copy of the executed agreement. If the agreement is a cancellable one, this second copy must be sent by post.

Improperly executed agreements

- If any of the documentation requirements are not complied with, the agreement is improperly executed and cannot be enforced by the creditor or owner without an order of the court (s 65 of the Consumer Credit Act 1974). Seizing possession of the goods amounts to enforcement.

- Generally, the court has a discretion to allow the creditor or owner to enforce the agreement, taking into account:

  - the culpability of the creditor or owner for the failure to comply;

  - the extent of prejudice, if any, to the debtor or hirer; and

- the powers of the court to reduce any sum payable by the debtor so as to undo any prejudice to him (s 127 of the Consumer Credit Act 1974).

- In three situations, however, the court may not grant an enforcement order:
  - where the agreement is a cancellable one and any copy given to the debtor omitted the notice of cancellation rights;
  - where the agreement is a cancellable one and a copy of the fully executed agreement has not been served on the debtor at some time before proceedings were commenced; and
  - where the debtor's or hirer's signature was not obtained on a document giving at least specified minimum information.

In *Dimond v Lovell* (2000), the House of Lords held that where the Act regarded an agreement as unenforceable, the agreement would be unenforceable even if this meant that the debtor was unjustly enriched. In *Wilson v First County Trust Ltd* (2003), the House of Lords confirmed this view, rejecting an argument that to render the agreement unenforceable breached the creditor's rights under the European Convention on Human Rights.

Documentation of security

- The Consumer Credit Act 1974 applies only to security as defined by the Act – namely, security 'provided by the debtor or hirer or at his request (express or implied), to secure the carrying out of the agreement' (s 189).

- If given by the debtor or hirer, it should be included within the regulated agreement.

- If given by someone else (for example, a guarantee given by a third party), that security should be signed by the person giving it (the surety) and by or on behalf of the creditor or owner. There are requirements as to the form it should be in. In addition, the surety should be given a copy of the regulated agreement.

- If these documentation requirements are not complied with, the security is improperly executed and is not enforceable against the surety without the creditor or owner obtaining a court order (s 105 of the Consumer Credit Act 1974). The court has a discretion as to whether to grant such an order (s 127 of the Consumer Credit Act 1974).

- The security cannot be enforced against the surety to any greater extent than the regulated agreement can be enforced against the debtor or hirer (s 113 of the Consumer Credit Act 1974).

Cancellable agreements

See flow chart on facing page.

Box 2

These agreements are not cancellable, but are subject to a special procedure whereby the creditor must give the debtor an advance copy of the prospective agreement and then allow the debtor a pre-signature consideration (cooling off) period of at least seven days (ss 58 and 61(2) of the Consumer Credit Act 1974).

Box 3

Where a dealer sells goods to a finance house which then contracts with the customer to supply the goods on *consumer hire* terms, the dealer will not be the agent of the finance company and any negotiations conducted by the dealer will not be 'antecedent negotiations'. Where the agreement made between the finance house and the customer is a *hire purchase*, *conditional sale* or *credit sale*, the negotiations conducted by

Flow chart to determine if agreement is cancellable within s 67 of the Consumer Credit Act 1974

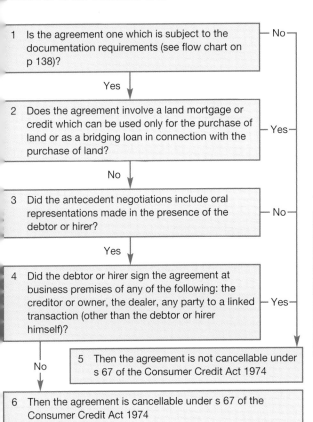

Cancellable agreements

143

Consumer credit IV

the dealer will be 'antecedent negotiations' (s 56 of the Consumer Credit Act 1974).

Box 5

An agreement may of course be cancellable under other legislation, including the Consumer Protection (Cancellation of Contracts Concluded away from Business Premises) Regulations 1987, which provide a cancellation period of seven days to a consumer who enters a contract as a result of doorstep canvassing. The 1987 regulations do not apply to any agreement which is cancellable under the Consumer Credit Act 1974.

Cancellation period

The debtor has the right to cancel a cancellable agreement at any time up to the end of the fifth day after he receives (by post) his copy of the executed agreement (or his notice of cancellation rights) (s 68 of the Consumer Credit Act 1974). If he posts it in time, that is sufficient (s 69(7) of the Consumer Credit Act 1974). The notice of cancellation served by the debtor need not be in any particular form so long as it is in writing.

Effect of cancellation (ss 69–73 of the Consumer Credit Act 1974)

Service of the notice of cancellation operates to cancel the cancellable agreement and also any linked transaction. The detailed effect of this cancellation depends upon the type of agreement.

Debtor–creditor–supplier and consumer hire agreements

(a) The debtor or hirer must return the goods (if any) which he has received under the agreement. However, he may refuse to do so until he is repaid such money as he is entitled to.

b) The debtor or hirer ceases to be liable to make payments and is entitled to the return of all money paid by him under the agreement.

c) The debtor or hirer is entitled to the return of any fees (in excess of £5) paid to a credit broker.

d) The debtor or hirer may have returned to him any goods he gave in part-exchange. If he does not get them back in substantially the same condition within ten days of cancellation, he is entitled to be repaid their part-exchange allowance.

e) By way of exception to (a) above, the debtor does not have to return any goods that were supplied to meet an emergency, or have been consumed before cancellation, or are perishable or have been incorporated into other property which is not the subject of the cancelled transaction(s).

f) By way of exception to (b) above, the debtor must, despite the cancellation, pay for: (i) any work done or goods supplied to meet an emergency; and (ii) any goods which the debtor has incorporated into some other property which is not subject to the cancelled transaction(s).

Other regulated consumer credit agreements

Despite cancellation, the agreement continues in force as regards the repayment of credit and interest. However, no interest is payable in respect of any of the credit which the debtor repays within one month of cancellation (or, if later, the date for payment of the first instalment under the agreement).

18 Agency and connected lender liability

Agency

At common law, in the triangular transaction, the dealer is not the agent of the finance house (see p 128). That is true whether the agreement that the finance house makes with the customer is a hire purchase, a simple hire agreement or even a loan agreement.

In the case of a regulated agreement, the position is reversed by s 56 of the Consumer Credit Act 1974 in respect of debtor–creditor–supplier agreements, but not where the agreement made between the customer and the finance house is a consumer hire agreement. Thus, during antecedent negotiations which lead to a regulated debtor–creditor–supplier agreement, the dealer is agent of the finance house. The fact that the dealer (retailer) is agent of the finance company means that the debtor can hold the finance company liable for misrepresentations made by the dealer. Also, money paid to the dealer will be regarded as paid to the finance company and notice given to the dealer will be notice to the finance company. This statutory agency arises, *inter alia*, in the case of regulated agreements of the following types:

- hire purchase;
- conditional sale;
- credit sale;
- loan; and
- credit card.

The first three of these types of agreement are always debtor–creditor–supplier agreements. The last two, however, may or may not be.

Loans

As far as loans are concerned, a debtor–creditor–supplier agreement might occur where, for example, a double glazing company offers the householder credit facilities to enable the customer to buy the double glazing. It may turn out that the credit facilities amount in fact to an opportunity to take a loan

om a finance house with which the double glazing company
as arrangements. In that case, during the antecedent
egotiations, the double glazing company's salesman is an
gent not just for the double glazing company, but also for the
nance house. That is the effect of s 56. Where, however, a
onsumer goes off on his own initiative and obtains a loan from
 finance house (for example, his own bank) to enable him to
uy goods or services, that loan agreement will not be a debtor–
reditor–supplier agreement because it is not made under
rrangements between the bank and the supplier of the goods
r services. In that situation, the retailer is not agent of the bank.

Credit cards

he following table indicates when a card is such that the
etailer is agent of the creditor (that is, the credit card issuer).

Card	Retailer agent of card issuer?	Why/why not?
Debit card (for example, Delta or Switch) used to pay from a current account in credit	No	Not a 'credit' agreement
Debit card (for example, Delta or Switch) used to pay from a current account in overdraft	No	Not a debtor–creditor–supplier agreement
Charge card (for example, Diners Club) where each periodical account is to be paid in a single payment	No	An exempt agreement and therefore not regulated by the Consumer Credit Act 1974
Credit card (for example, Barclaycard) used to draw cash (for example, from ATM) on credit and the cash is then used to pay the retailer	No	The credit card agreement is a multiple agreement. When used this way, it is a debtor–creditor agreement

Card	Retailer agent of card issuer?	Why/why not?
Credit card used as means of paying retailer	Yes	Assuming the card allows the balance to be paid off in more than one payment, it is a debtor–creditor–supplier agreement when used in this way

Section 75 of the Consumer Credit Act 1974

This section created what is known as connected lender liability. When s 75 applies, it makes the creditor jointly and severally liable with the supplier for misrepresentations and breaches of contract by the supplier. This gives the debtor the option of bringing the claim against the creditor instead of the supplier. This can be of great advantage to the debtor where the supplier is: (a) insolvent; (b) difficult to trace; or (c) simply unwilling to accept the claim.

In *Office of Fair Trading v Lloyds TSB Bank plc* (2004) it was held that s 75 does not apply to foreign transactions.

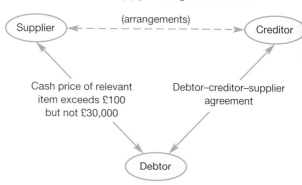

ow chart to determine if s 75 applies

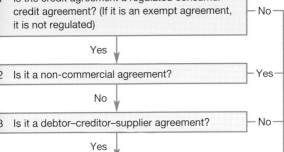

1	Is the credit agreement a regulated consumer credit agreement? (If it is an exempt agreement, it is not regulated)

— No —

Yes ↓

2	Is it a non-commercial agreement?

— Yes —

No ↓

3	Is it a debtor–creditor–supplier agreement?

— No —

Yes ↓

4	Are the creditor and the supplier one and the same person?

— Yes —

No ↓

5	Does the claim relate to a single item to which the supplier attached a cash price of £100 or less?

— Yes —

No ↓

6	Does the claim relate to a single item to which the supplier attached a cash price of more than £30,000?

— Yes —

No ↓

7	Then s 75 does not apply

8	Then s 75 applies and the debtor can claim against the creditor or the supplier for an misrepresentation or breach of contract by the supplier

Section 75

151

Lender liability

Boxes 1–3

In the table relating to credit cards on pp 149–150, in the first four examples, the answer to whether the retailer was agent of the card issuer was 'No'. In those examples, the answer to the question of whether s 75 applies would also be 'No' – and for exactly the same reasons. In the fifth and final example in that table, the answer would be 'Yes', but only if the cash price of the item exceeded £100 and did not exceed £30,000.

Box 4

There is no point in making – and s 75 does not make – the creditor and supplier jointly and severally liable where they are in fact the same person. That means that s 75 never applies to hire purchase, conditional sale or credit sale agreements. This is because, even in the triangular transaction, the finance house buys the goods and then contracts to supply them to the debtor (on hire purchase, etc, terms). Thus, the finance house is the supplier. If the goods prove not to be of satisfactory quality, the debtor's claim is against the finance company anyway.

Box 8

If the debtor has a claim against the supplier for misrepresentation or breach of contract, s 75 enables the debtor to bring a 'like claim' against the creditor. Apparently, that means that if he has a claim to rescind the supply agreement, he has a right to rescind the credit agreement (*United Dominions Trust v Taylor* (1980)).

There is some doubt whether s 75 applies where a second authorised card holder has used the card.

19 Consumer credit – rights of the parties

The following table summarises *some* of the respective rights of the debtor and creditor which exist, or may exist, depending on the terms of the agreement. The debtor's rights are largely spelt out in the Consumer Credit Act 1974. The creditor's rights will usually be spelt out in the agreement.

Debtor's rights	Creditor's rights
To make early repayment and earn rebate of credit charges (s 94)	To be paid (repaid) according to the terms of the agreement
To receive default notice before creditor able to take precipitate knock-out action (s 87)	To terminate the agreement
Not to be obliged to pay default interest at a rate higher than the APR payable under the agreement as a whole (s 93)	To repossess the goods
To re-open an extortionate credit bargain (ss 137–40)	To enforce security
To have debtor's heirs able to take over the agreement (s 86)	To be compensated for misuse of credit facilities up to a limit
To apply for a time order (s 129)	

Default in payment

The debtor defaulting in making the payments due under the agreement is easily the most common event to cause the rights of the parties to be actively considered. There could be several rights of the creditor which will arise in such an eventuality:

- Claim the arrears. The creditor is immediately entitled to bring proceedings to enforce payment of instalments which have fallen due. The agreement may provide that interest is payable on the arrears until they are paid. If so, the rate of the interest charged must not exceed the rate of the APR payable under the agreement as a whole.

The creditor will have the right to terminate the agreement if:

- the breach amounts to a repudiation of the agreement;
- the agreement states that prompt payment of sums due is 'of the essence' of the agreement (*Lombard North Central v Butterworth* (1988)); or
- the agreement expressly gives that right.

The creditor may well have the right to repossess the goods (for example, upon termination of a hire purchase agreement).

The creditor will have the right to activate an accelerated payments clause, if the agreement gives him that right.

Similarly, the creditor will have the right to enforce security.

All of these rights of the creditor, apart from (a), are dramatic and likely to be final so far as the debtor is concerned. Thus, in those cases, but not in the case of (a), the creditor is not entitled to exercise any of these rights without first serving on the debtor a default notice (s 87 of the Consumer Credit Act 1974) giving the debtor at least seven days' notice. If the debtor makes good his default (pays off all his arrears) before expiry of the default notice, the debtor is deemed not to have defaulted at all. Even if he does not make good his default, the debtor may apply for a time order.

Termination and accelerated payments clauses

These are often to be found in credit agreements.

The termination clause is likely to be found in hire purchase and conditional sale agreements, where the result of termination is that in principle the creditor is entitled to the return of the goods.

The accelerated payments clause is likely to be found in these or in any other credit agreement which provides for repayment by regular instalments. Once it has been effectively activated, an accelerated payments clause means that the whole outstanding balance becomes due immediately, that is, that the payments that had been expected to fall due over the coming months and years are all payable immediately. The creditor is required to deduct a rebate of charges to reflect the fact that payment is required earlier. Nevertheless, for a debtor who has already got into arrears, insisting that he pays all the outstanding instalments immediately is likely to be an impossible demand and may push him into bankruptcy. Thus, the debtor faced with such a demand may ask the court to grant a time order.

Table comparing effect of termination clause and accelerated payments clause in a hire purchase agreement

Termination clause	Accelerated payments clause
Debtor has to surrender the goods and never becomes owner	Debtor becomes owner immediately and retains the goods
Debtor cannot recover payments already made and has to pay arrears already fallen due. He may have to pay a further sum to the creditor depending on the value of the goods when returned to the creditor	Debtor cannot recover payments already made, remains liable to pay arrears and must pay immediately the whole of the outstanding balance of future instalments
Debtor will be liable to pay default interest on arrears at a rate not exceeding the APR payable under the agreement	Debtor will be liable to pay default interest on arrears at a rate not exceeding the APR payable under the agreement, but will be entitled to a rebate of charges in respect of future instalments paid early as a result of the clause

Time order (s 129 of the Consumer Credit Act 1974)

At any time after a default notice has been served, or in any proceedings to enforce a regulated agreement against him, the debtor can apply to the court for a time order. Often, this occurs after a default notice has expired and the creditor is claiming one of the remedies listed above. The choice before the court is:

either

> to allow the creditor the remedy sought (for example, activation of an acceleration payments clause or immediate termination of the agreement, coupled in the latter case perhaps with repossession of the goods);

or

> to grant the debtor a time order under s 129.

The time order in effect allows the debtor a second chance, an extended time in which to make payments that are overdue. In the case of a hire purchase or conditional sale agreement, it can alter (that is, extend) the future repayment pattern as well as allow extra time for payment of sums that have already fallen due. The court will not grant a time order without hearing evidence of the debtor's means and will then not grant a time order unless it thinks that the debtor has some reasonable chance of being able to make the payment according to the terms of the time order.

Protected goods (ss 90–91 of the Consumer Credit Act 1974)

These provisions apply only to regulated hire purchase and conditional sale agreements. They apply to these agreements because there is a chance that after the debtor's default the creditor will serve a default notice and that the default notice will expire without the debtor having paid off his arrears. That being so, the creditor may then lawfully terminate the agreement and he can do this simply by giving written notice of it. Upon termination of a hire purchase or conditional sale agreement, the creditor is in principle entitled to the return of the goods (which, of course, are his) (*Bowmakers v Barnett Instruments* (1945)).

The protected goods provisions are designed to prevent the creditor simply helping himself to the goods before the debtor has had a chance to appear in court and, perhaps, apply for a time order. Thus, where the goods are protected goods, the creditor is not entitled to take possession of the goods from the debtor without his consent unless he has received a court order. He is equally prevented from seizing the goods, without the debtor's consent, from anyone to whom the debtor has passed possession temporarily, as could happen, for example, if it is a car and he has let his wife drive it or has left it at the garage for servicing (*Bentinck v Cromwell Engineering* (1971)). If the creditor does take possession of protected goods, then unless the debtor gave his consent to the repossession at the time of the repossession, the debtor is released from any obligation to make further payments under the agreement and is entitled to be repaid all payments he has already made under it (s 91).

Goods are protected goods if:

- the debtor is in breach of the agreement; and
- the debtor has paid or tendered at least one-third of the total price payable under the agreement; and
- the property in the goods remains in the creditor.

Unauthorised use of credit facilities

- Generally, the debtor is not liable to the creditor for unauthorised use of credit facilities by other people (s 83 of the Consumer Credit Act 1974).

- Section 84 of the Consumer Credit Act 1974 provides an exception for unauthorised use of credit tokens (for example, credit cards) and allows the debtor to be made liable for up to £50 in respect of each time the card falls into unauthorised hands.

Extortionate credit bargains (ss 137–40 of the Consumer Credit Act 1974)

The court can re-open any personal credit agreement on the grounds that it was an extortionate credit bargain. It will be extortionate if: (a) it demands payments that are grossly exorbitant; or (b) it in some other way grossly contravenes ordinary principles of fair dealing.

The usual comparison to be used by the courts when an agreement is alleged to amount to an extortionate credit bargain is to look at the interest rate charged generally in the market in respect of the same type of agreement at the time the agreement was made.

Provisions specific to regulated hire purchase and conditional sale agreements

- The *protected goods provisions* (above) are specific to these kinds of agreements.

- Also, when making a *time order*, the court can make an order granting extra time for payment of *instalments that have not yet fallen due*. Again, this particular provision is confined to these kinds of agreement.

- The debtor is given a *statutory right to terminate* the agreement by giving written notice at any time before the whole of the total price falls due (s 99 of the Consumer Credit Act 1974). Thus, if an accelerated payments clause has been activated (that is, the appropriate default notice has been served and expired without the debtor making good his default), the whole of the outstanding balance will have fallen due and thus the debtor will by then have lost his s 99 right

159

Regulated hire purchases

Consumer credit V

of termination (*Wadham Stringer v Meaney* (1981)). If the
debtor exercises this right of termination:

- he becomes liable to return the goods;
- he will sacrifice all payments already made under the
  agreement;
- he will remain liable to pay all arrears that had fallen due
  before he exercised his right of termination; and
- he may be required by the court to pay a further amount
  to bring up the sums at (b) and (c) to half of the total price
  payable under the agreement.

The court has power to make a *return order* requiring the
debtor to return the goods to the creditor (s 133 of the
Consumer Credit Act 1974). This power will usually be used
where the debtor has got into arrears, and a default notice
has been served and expired without the debtor paying off
the arrears. The choice facing the court may be either to
grant the return order requiring the debtor to return the
goods or to grant the debtor a time order.

The court has power to suspend the operation of any order
it makes or to make it conditional upon some event (s 135 of
the Consumer Credit Act 1974). Thus, the court could, at the
same time, make: (a) a time order; and (b) an order for the
debtor to return the goods but suspend the operation of the
return order until such time as the debtor defaults on the
payments as required by the time order.

As an alternative to a return order or a time order, the court
can, where the goods are divisible, make a *transfer order*,
transferring ownership of some of the goods to the debtor
and requiring him to return the rest of them to the creditor
(s 133 of the Consumer Credit Act 1974). This is possible
only where the debtor has paid both: (a) that proportion of
the total price attributable to the goods being transferred to
his ownership; and (b) a certain amount more, equivalent
to one quarter of the rest of the total price.